FALL TO GRACE

Also by Jay Bakker

Son of a Preacher Man: My Search for Grace in the Shadows

FALL TO GRACE

A REVOLUTION OF GOD, SELF & SOCIETY

JAY BAKKER
with MARTIN EDLUND

NEW YORK   BOSTON   NASHVILLE

Unless otherwise noted, Scriptures are taken from the *Holy Bible*, New Living Translation, copyright © 1996. Used by permission of Tyndale House Publishers, Inc., Wheaton, Illinois 60189. All rights reserved.

Scriptures noted NIV are taken from the HOLY BIBLE: NEW INTERNATIONAL VERSION®. Copyright © 1973, 1978, 1984 by International Bible Society. Used by permission of Zondervan Publishing House. All rights reserved.

Scriptures noted KJV are taken from the King James Version of the Bible.

FaithWords
Hachette Book Group
237 Park Avenue
New York, NY 10017
www.faithwords.com

Printed in the United States of America

First Edition: January 2011
10 9 8 7 6 5 4 3 2 1

FaithWords is a division of Hachette Book Group, Inc. The FaithWords name and logo are trademarks of Hachette Book Group, Inc.

The publisher is not responsible for websites (or their content) that are not owned by the publisher.

Library of Congress Cataloging-in-Publication Data
Bakker, Jay.
    Fall to grace : a revolution of God, self and society / Jay Bakker. —1st ed.
        p. cm.
    Summary: "Jay Bakker explores the radical, transformative, and inclusive nature at the heart of Jesus's message: grace"—Provided by the publisher.
    ISBN 978-0-446-53950-0
    1. Christian life. 2. Grace (Theology) I. Title.
    BV4501.3.B3552 2011
234—dc22

2010020611

*This book is dedicated to the memory of Tammy Faye
and the new life of Maret Bassett Edlund.*

Nothing else in the world matters but the kindness of grace, God's gift to suffering mortals.

—*Jack Kerouac, 1961*

Contents

CONTENTS

Introduction

The Grace Revolution

I've been around churches my whole life, yet I didn't discover grace—true grace, revolutionary grace—until I was twenty years old. Even then, it has taken me fourteen years to really get my head around it and begin to understand its implications.

Sure, I had heard people talk and sing about grace in church. At times, it seemed that they talked of little else. But as far as I could tell, the word didn't *mean* anything. It was an empty shell; a verbal tic ("grace be with you"); a lyric in a song—there certainly wasn't anything "amazing" about it. But make no mistake: This soft-sounding concept has the power to change the world. Grace saved my life; it can revolutionize yours.

Grace is so poorly understood that it's worth defining right up front. *Grace* literally means "unmerited favor." It is the idea that we receive salvation as a gift from God through Christ's sacrifice on the cross. Not as something we've earned. Not because of what we do (or don't do). Not because we pass some kind of test. Just because God loved us enough to redeem us through His Son.

Grace is that simple. Grace is that complicated.

Grace has enormous consequences for our faith, our lives, and our world. What changes when you embrace grace? Everything. You begin to love God instead of fearing God. You begin to trust Christ in your life and in the lives of others instead of judging everyone (especially yourself) by impossible standards. With grace comes the freedom to fall short. You can deepen your relationship with God even when you fail—especially when you fail. With grace comes the inspiration to start living out the crazy, impossible teachings of Christ: to love God above all else; to love your neighbor as yourself; to love even your enemies.

The power of this idea to transform our lives is why I call grace "revolutionary." It's a revolution in three parts: first, a revolution in our understanding of God and religion; second, a revolution in our understanding of ourselves as God's children; and finally, through grace, a revolution of our relationship with other people and, ultimately, the world as a whole.

The turning point in my understanding of grace came when a friend convinced me to spend time with the writings of the apostle Paul, especially his Letter to the Galatians. Galatians is now my favorite book in the Bible (and not just because it's one of the shortest, although as someone who is severely dyslexic I appreciate that too). If it hadn't been for Paul's message of grace, I would have drunk myself into the ground before my thirtieth birthday. For years leading up to that point, it had been Jay Bakker vs. Jack Daniel's in a no-holds-barred old-fashioned bar fight. Jack was kicking my ass before grace stepped in to stop the fight.

Part of what appeals to me about Paul's letters is that they were written at a time closer to Christ's earthly life than any other books of the Bible. Biblical scholars tell us that Paul's letters were written roughly twenty years after Jesus died—a full twenty to twenty-five years before even the Gospels of Matthew, Mark, Luke, and John that record Christ's life and words. I also like that Paul himself was something of an outsider to the religious establishment of his time. He was the original "grace revolutionary."

Today we think of him as Saint Paul, the most prolific writer and the deepest thinker of the New Testament. But he wasn't one of the original twelve apostles, and because of his uncompromising commitment to grace, the founders of the church were always a bit suspicious of him. If Peter was "the Rock" on which the church was founded, Paul was the rock in the shoe of the early church; thank God his writings are still here to remind and aggravate us every step of the way on our journey.

I often hear Christians complain about how unpopular the church is today. They struggle to find or define Christ's relevance amid the vogue of atheism, New Age–ism, and à la carte religious practice. The numbers bear out their fears: according to the 2008 American Religious Identification Survey, the number of Americans who claim no religious affiliation whatsoever has almost doubled since 1990, from 8 to 15 percent.[1]

I believe grace is the answer. It has much to offer a society that has been turned off by Christianity. It can heal the wounds of people who have been battered and scarred by their run-ins with the church. It healed mine.

For non-Christians—people of other faiths or no faith at all—grace offers a message of tolerance and understanding. It shows a Christianity that is richer and gentler than the distorted parody presented by hellfire preachers and the politicized faith of the religious Right. Grace goes beyond mere tolerance: it calls us to think of ourselves as all belonging to one body, the body of Christ.

Paradoxically, devout Christians may find it hardest to accept grace because it flies in the face of so much of what we may have learned in church. It contradicts much of what passes for "Christianity" in popular culture today. (In the wrong hands, even grace gets twisted into a negative concept: proof of human worthlessness and a gift given only to the "elect.") For the faithful, I hope this book will deepen your understanding as well as your faith, and help open your eyes to the profoundly loving relationships that are available with God and your fellow man.

This book is about fulfilling that revolutionary potential. It's about helping us to live gracefully. To live grace. Fully.

Grace is our destination. Paul is our guide. Galatians is the tattered road map we'll occasionally pull from the glove box for reference. Let the journey begin.

FALL TO GRACE

Chapter 1

Free-Fallin'

We are punished by our sins, not for them.

—*Elbert Hubbard*

You know you've reached a new level of fame in American culture (or infamy) when there's a casting call to play you in a movie.

In my case, it was a second-rate made-for-TV movie called *Fall from Grace*, starring Kevin Spacey as my dad and Bernadette Peters—face painted like the side of a barn—as my mom. Somewhere in Hollywood a bunch of chubby white kids lined up, hoping to get their big break playing the part of little Jamie Charles Bakker, son of disgraced televangelists Jim and Tammy Faye.

What those other kids might not have realized was that being the son of the picture-perfect Christian family was a role for me too. Twice a week I would don a child-sized suit, tame my cowlick, and brandish my jack-o'-lantern grin for an audience of millions on my parents' Praise the Lord (PTL) television ministry.

The network's supporters were my extended family. All through grade school, my yearbook picture (no matter how humiliating) was mailed to six hundred thousand PTL faithful around the world. They knew of my birth even before my dad did. He was on the air preaching when the producers flashed the words "It's a boy! It's a boy!" across the bottom of the screen like a severe-weather warning. On December 18, 1975, Hurricane Jay made landfall.

For those readers who don't know my family story, or have assigned those memories to the junk pile of 1980s trivia, let me lay a little groundwork here. It's not that I take pleasure in retreading this territory (believe me, I don't). But I do think it's important that you understand what I've lived through to learn grace.

My family set the standard for televised crack-ups. Before O.J. on the interstate, before Michael Jackson dangled babies over balconies, before Britney went all bald and strange, there was the Jim and Tammy Faye "mascara meltdown." But prior to being pariahs my parents were pop-culture pioneers. They were the first people to bring down-home, family-friendly Christian worship into America's living rooms through television. They paved the way for the best-selling mega-church stars of today. For good or ill, it all started with my mom and dad.

And it all started humbly enough. In 1964, my parents made their first appearance on the Christian Broadcasting Network, the station of future Christian television mogul Pat Robertson. They debuted with a kids' show featuring handmade puppets: Susie Moppet (a Porky Pig bubble-bath cap refashioned with braids, voiced by my mom) and Allie the Alligator (a leopard-print sock with teeth, voiced by Dad) would sing Christian songs and explain God's Word.

One thing led to another, and by the mid-1980s my parents owned one of only four satellite TV networks in the world, along with a sprawling theme park and the largest TV ministry the world had ever witnessed. At its height, PTL was carried on twelve hundred cable systems around the globe, broadcasting into more than thirteen million homes.

Dad became a global figure—a new breed of Christian businessman and a friend to presidents and movie stars. He convinced himself that it was all in keeping with God's plan. He told *Time* magazine in 1986 that if Jesus were alive today, "he'd have to be on TV. That would be the only way he could reach the people he loves."[1]

Dad preached a soft version of the prosperity gospel, one that said: *Do good and you'll do well—then give some back.* He didn't run commercials on the network, so his whole ministry became a kind of on-air appeal. He was constantly raising money to keep PTL going—and growing. At its height, PTL had to raise $500,000 per day to keep the lights on. (Dad would later admit that fund-raising got in the way of his relationship with God and led to some of the decisions that would be his undoing.)

PTL spawned a family-friendly theme park, Heritage USA, which my parents constructed across an expansive 2,300-acre campus in Fort Mill, South Carolina. Only Disneyland and Disney World drew bigger crowds.

The main difference was that everything in our magical

kingdom was Christian-themed. Dad had the childhood home of his hero Billy Graham relocated to the Heritage grounds. There were daily Passion plays and a "Heavenly Fudge Factory." There was even a "Noah's Toy Shop" (run by a guy actually named Noah) that sold disciple action figures and other Bible-themed toys.

My personal favorite was the "Armor of God," a child's bodysuit and arsenal of plastic weaponry that was inspired by a quote from the book of Ephesians. With the "Shield of Faith" in one hand and the "Sword of the Spirit" in the other, I ran around Heritage USA like it was my own personal fiefdom. But even the molded-plastic "Breastplate of Righteousness" was no protection against what was coming next...

The Crack-up

Both the rise and the fall of PTL reinforced the idea that God metes out rewards and punishment based on behavior. For the longest time it seemed that God wanted us to succeed. Everything went right for the Bakkers. Until it didn't.

The cracks began to show in January 1987, when my mom accidentally overdosed. I was eleven years old. We checked her into the Betty Ford Center (thus beginning a proud tradition for the Bakker family), only to discover that she was addicted to enough over-the-counter drugs to tranquilize a gorilla. She'd been using them to cope with the stresses of business and stardom.

The story was too tantalizing for the press to resist: the perky Christian poster mom was a drug addict! The media descended on us like something out of Revelation. Swarms of cameras surrounded the clinic. Media vans staked out our home. Photographers rented U-Haul trucks to use as step stools so they could take pictures over the walls and through the windows of our compound. The white sheets we hung in the windows to obscure their view did little to discourage them.

From that moment on, we were no longer hosts of our own TV show but unwilling stars in everyone else's. Being a Bakker was a prime-time media spectacle, one we couldn't turn off.

Things went from bad to worse in 1987 when the *Charlotte Observer* broke the news that my dad had had an affair seven years prior with a comely Christian secretary named Jessica Hahn. The story was everywhere: CNN, *Nightline*, Johnny Carson. My parents forbade my sister, Tammy Sue, and me to turn on the TV, but that didn't stop us from catching Phil Hartman's devastating imitation of my father on *Saturday Night Live* (which included a scolding at the hands of Dana Carvey's "Church Lady").

Adding a sleazy taint to an already humiliating affair, it came out that someone from PTL had paid Hahn hundreds of thousands of dollars in hush money to keep the secret all those years. If God had favored us before, He now had clearly changed His mind.

In an attempt to save PTL, my father turned the network over temporarily (or so he thought) to Jerry Falwell. Falwell had advance knowledge that the Hahn story was going to break and promised to look after things while my father rode out the storm. The man he chose to shepherd his empire turned out to be a wolf. Falwell immediately began denouncing my parents from their own pulpit. Others joined in on the chorus. "Jim Bakker is a cancer in the body of Christ," proclaimed Jimmy Swaggart to Larry King on CNN.[2] Pat Robertson, who had helped launch my parents' career, would also play a part in its undoing. They got their just deserts, he pronounced.

Falwell accused Dad of everything he could think of: not just thievery and having "an unrepentant heart," but of homosexuality too. As you can imagine, that last charge was especially damning in evangelical circles. We lost the TV network, Heritage USA, and our home (which was owned in the name of PTL). To add insult to injury, Falwell auctioned off what he considered our most humiliating personal items in front of the media: a mini go-kart, my parents' bed, and the notorious "air-conditioned" doghouse.

From the perspective of an eleven-year-old boy, the free fall was dizzying. One minute I was the scion of a famous family. The next I was a social leper with the most notorious last name in Christendom (besides Iscariot). I was so radioactive that my friends were literally forbidden to play with me.

Unfortunately, my faith was cold comfort in those days. My parents weren't fire-and-brimstone types, not by any means. (They signed off every episode of their show with the catchphrase "God loves you. He really, really does.") But they did subscribe to the standard-issue Southern evangelical beliefs of the day. Heaven and hell were the carrot and the stick of our faith. It was *turn or burn, baby*. Either you followed the rules or you went straight to H-E-double-hockey-sticks.

I didn't have grace to lean on then. I didn't know where these rules came from, or what to do with them. Despite spending my whole life in church, I had hardly opened a Bible. I hadn't read Christ's words highlighted in red, let alone Paul's letters to the Romans or Galatians—books that might have given me some comfort and perspective on grace.

My family crises were compounded by my problems with classwork in junior high. I had severe dyslexia, a condition that would go undiagnosed until seven years later, long after I'd dropped out of school. It made learning virtually impossible for me. And when I couldn't keep up, I gave up and did what any frustrated son of fallen televangelists would do...I rebelled.

In cigarettes and wine coolers I finally found something at which I could excel. I was only twelve years old, but they were easy enough to come by. When I started partying, I told myself, *I'll just have wine coolers. It's cool. Jesus had wine.* But I always feared there was more to it. You see, the way I was brought up, sipping a wine cooler wasn't just a youthful indiscretion—I was sipping strawberry-flavored hellfire!

It seemed there was always someone around to remind me of the flames nipping at my heels. On one occasion, I was at an outdoor party in high school when a girl I went to Christian summer camp with drove by and saw me holding a bottle. She pulled over the truck she was driving, rolled down the window, and yelled: "I knew you wouldn't last!" It was straight out of the movie *Saved!* Today I have some appreciation for the complicated mix of guilt and anguish that drives someone to lash out as she did, but back then it was just a punch in the gut.

It's not that I didn't try to get right with God. I just didn't know where to start. Throughout my teenage years I got saved what seemed like every other week. I'd come down to the altar call with the rest of the guilt-stricken and confused junior high kids, bow my head, close my eyes, and *shazam!*—wait for God to transform me.

It never lasted, of course. Not for very long, anyway. Before I knew it, I'd do/think/feel something sinful and start looking for the next opportunity to bleach my soul clean. Instead of bringing me back into the fold, my guilt—reinforced by the judgment of those around me—drove me further from the church.

If a lousy Bartles & Jaymes wine cooler was all it took to separate me from God, then I was gonna accept my one-way ticket to hell... *Reserve me a seat in the bar car!*

I now realize that this was the classic dynamic of religious law at work. It wasn't the Ten Commandments per se, but it was a set of religious rules nonetheless: *do's* and *don'ts* that would decide whether God's love and Christ's sacrifice applied to me. (Or so I thought at the time.)

Hitting Bottom

If my struggles with school and faith weren't complicated enough, there was still more Bakker family fun to be had. In December 1988, almost two years after the outing of my dad's affair, a long-running federal investigation into the finances of Heritage USA went public. The accusation came down to overbooking: PTL had sold more lifetime memberships to Heritage USA—complete with the promise of three nights' lodging—than it could possibly accommodate at once. Dad was indicted on twenty-four counts of fraud and conspiracy.

The trial began with a bang in August 1989. Three days into it, my dad had a Xanax-fueled emotional breakdown in front of the press. Dad was paraded, sobbing and shackled, through a gauntlet of TV cameras to the mental ward. It may have been great television, but it was torture for me to watch.

United States vs. James O. Bakker was about more than one organization's sloppy accounting or one man's malfeasance (though there was plenty of both to go around). The whole era of televangelism was on trial, and my dad was already guilty in the highest court in the land: the court of public opinion. The judge (nicknamed "Maximum Bob" for his draconian sentencing) made it official when he sentenced my dad to forty-five years in prison. He would ultimately serve five, but it was long enough for my parents' marriage to unravel.

The very night of my dad's sentencing marked the beginning (or radical acceleration, anyway) of my own downward spiral. I was thirteen years old when some older kids decided to take pity on me and take me out partying. I never looked back. Wine coolers quickly gave way to stiffer stuff: vodka and Gatorade (bad combination), pot smoking, even gas huffing. By the time I dropped out of school in tenth grade I was punching above my weight (using acid, psychedelic mushrooms—whatever I could get my hands on). It went on like this for years.

Separation from my dad was my excuse for drinking, but

his release from prison five years later wasn't reason enough to quit. If anything, his being out made things harder as we tried to navigate new dimensions of our father-son relationship. A lot had changed in five years. When he went in, I was little Jamie Charles: thirteen, chunky, and scared to death of losing my dad. When he came out, I was Jay. Just Jay, thank you very much: eighteen, pierced, and a raging alcoholic. Needless to say, things didn't go smoothly between us.

Dad did what he could to steer me back toward Christianity. When all else failed, he shipped me off to Arizona to a young ministers training camp called Master's Commission. As advertised, it was all about control. They had been forewarned about what a hellion I was, so the counselors (all in their mid-twenties) mapped out roles for dealing with me: One person would be good cop; another the bad cop; a third the flirtatious fellow rebel. It was like a bad John Hughes movie, and I saw right through it.

I did meet two kindred spirits in the place, however, and we decided to break out together. Mike Wall was a tall, charismatic hard-core-punk kid; Kelli Miller, Mike's partner in crime, was a free-spirited hippie throwback. They had the idea of starting a ministry that would cater to skater and punk kids in a language and style they could understand. With me as the requisite skater brat, we had our outcast bases covered.

For a while, it worked like a dream. We bailed on Master's Commission and started putting on punk shows under the name Revolution Ministries, using great local Phoenix hard-core bands to attract a crowd. We took no small amount of pride in the fact that our preaching was the wildest part of the night. We had all sorts of antics: Mike would smash TVs with a sledgehammer; I'd pretend to puke onstage. We got ourselves banned by some local youth groups, which did wonders for our street cred.

I was in so much personal pain that I had no trouble relating to the suffering of the troubled teens our ministry attracted. Unfortunately, I wasn't ready to change. Not yet. I kept slipping back into old behaviors. I resumed partying with a vengeance and left Revolution behind. My "weekend benders" soon stretched from Wednesdays to Mondays. I began blacking out every time I drank.

If there was one thing I was sure of, it was that God was through with me: I had even failed at the burnout-and-misfit church!

Chapter 2

The Rising

Man is born broken. He lives by mending. The grace of God is glue.

—*Eugene O'Neill, American playwright*

My personal grace revolution didn't come in a blinding flash as it did for Paul. It was more gradual: a grace *evolution*. And it started only once I had bottomed out completely.

As strange as it sounds, I now look back on these events as growing pains of sorts. The end of innocence was the beginning of hard-won wisdom. Though the path would be twisted and difficult, these events set me on the road to discovering grace.

When I moved to Atlanta in 1995 to live with my friend Donnie Earl Paulk (D.E. for short), I was still running from my problems, still drinking like a fish. This was the second time I had landed on D.E.'s doorstep. A few years before, when my dad was transferred from a prison in Minnesota to one in Jesup, Georgia, the Paulk family let me move in with them so that I could visit my dad on weekends.

D.E. came from a clan of preachers too. His dad and uncle were both ministers at a big church called the Cathedral of the Holy Spirit (where we would have my mother's funeral service). Part of his father's claim to fame was that he was one of the few white pastors to march with Martin Luther King Jr. in the 1960s. But by the time I arrived to live with them, they were entangled in their own local scandal. They had media camped outside their house. It felt just like home!

Despite the unwanted attention, the Paulk house was a refuge for me, a port in the storm. D.E. had become my surrogate big brother. With him it was different. He didn't condemn me when I screwed up or command me to quit drinking. He didn't try to change me. He certainly didn't invoke God's name to try to scare me straight like so many Christians had before. He just made sure I didn't hurt myself.

When I went out to bars, D.E. would sip a seltzer and sit with me. When I blacked out, he made sure I got home safe. When I showed up to the house at sunrise too drunk to fit the keys into the lock, he would let me in without comment or complaint. It was like having my own personal guardian angel.

D.E.'s constant companionship gave us plenty of time to talk, and faith (or the lack thereof) was a frequent topic of conversation—and confrontation. We agreed on very little at first. D.E. would describe these beautiful things about God's unwavering love. How it wasn't up to us to succeed or fail in earning God's grace. That Christ accomplished our salvation on the cross.

I thought he was full of it and told him so: "Whatever helps you sleep at night, buddy," I said.

What was I supposed to think? The Christianity D.E. described bore little resemblance to the church I grew up around. What about all those rules I was breaking? What about sin and hell? What about all those strawberry-flavored Bartles & Jaymes wine coolers I drank as a teenager? *You think God doesn't care about that?!*

Our conversations went something like this:

"God hates me. I'm a mistake," I would start out.

"Jay, you're full of it," D.E. would answer. "You're trying to earn your salvation instead of recognizing that Christ did it for you when He sacrificed Himself on the cross. God doesn't care if you drink. God loves you right where you are."

Rinse and repeat.

I wasn't buying it. Grace sounded like a cop-out to me, an excuse to sin. I didn't realize that I had a living, breathing example of grace in practice right in front of me in the form of D.E.'s patient friendship. Finally, after months of this, I ran out of retorts and decided to play my trump card: "All right, prove it," I said, thinking I was calling his bluff. "Show me in the Bible."

That's when D.E. convinced me to start reading the letters of Paul: especially Galatians, Ephesians, and Romans. What I found was so compelling that it inspired a period of intensive study in religious law—the rules and regulations that, back in Jesus' time, one was supposed to follow to earn

God's favor and escape His wrath. I researched where those rules and regulations came from and what they mean for us today. As I came to understand their historical and biblical origins, I began to realize that the Kool-Aid I drank in church and youth groups was spiked, that it blinded me to grace. I began to recognize how these old rules get updated to frighten and intimidate each generation anew, how they continue to drive many of us to feel we've failed completely and turn away from the church, and even God.

You might say the scales fell from my eyes. Who knew that grace was right there in black and white, that the Bible actually held the answer to my doubts about Christianity. As it turned out, the best defense against all those Bible-thumpers who were driving people like me away from the church was right there in Paul's letters (in the Bible!) all along.

Over time, many of the Scriptures that I'd been blind to came to vivid life:

> We all can be saved . . . no matter who we are or what we have done. For all have sinned; all fall short of God's glorious standard. Yet now God in his gracious kindness declares us not guilty. He has done this through Christ Jesus, who has freed us by taking away our sins. (Romans 3:22–24)

> You can't take credit for this; it is a gift from God. Salvation is not a reward for the good things we have done, so none of us can boast about it. (Ephesians 2:8–9)

Christ has accomplished the whole purpose of the law.
All who believe in him are made right with God. (Romans 10:4)

Paul's message wasn't about guilt and punishment. It was
about acceptance; it was about forgiveness; and it applied to
me! What I felt instinctively about God—that He must be
loving and understanding of human frailty—was right after
all. Where had Paul been all my life?

Grace Fiend

I became a grace convert. A grace fiend, even. I couldn't
get enough of the stuff. I pumped D.E. for knowledge every
chance I got. I'd pepper him up with questions into the wee
hours of the night, until he fell asleep midsentence.

One night, still on a grace high, I called my dad and
woke him up.

"Dad, God really loves us!" I said excitedly.

"I know, son," he answered, "but sometimes I have trouble believing it."

They say a sober man's thoughts are a drunken man's
words. There is little question what was on my mind in
those days. I was still getting drunk, but instead of chasing
girls or getting into fights, I spouted grace to anyone who
would listen (and to many who wouldn't). If I saw a guy
with a Jesus tattoo at a bar, I'd pounce: "Hey, cool tattoo,
man. You a Christian? Yeah, well, do you know about grace?
That's right, Jesus loves us even if we're drunk. Isn't that
awesome? Let me get the next round..."

I didn't win any converts in those days, but I did manage to convince myself. Bit by bit, my guilt was starting to bleed away.

This was a critical turning point in my own personal grace revolution. I could have stopped and sunk into my spiritual La-Z-Boy, bottle in hand, comforted by the knowledge that God loved me no matter how much Jack I drank or what other misadventures I got into. I could have stalled out right then and there. Fortunately, grace gave me the motivation to keep going.

The first step was realizing that drinking wasn't the answer to my misery, it was part of the problem. I began to see the wisdom in the Elbert Hubbard line (often paraphrased by Mike Ness, front man of my favorite band, Social Distortion): "We are punished by our sins, not for them." My drinking was a self-inflected wound, friendly fire. It was hurting only me. If I really wanted to experience the fullness of God's grace, I would have to give it up.

I had tried to quit before, of course, but this time was different. For once, I wasn't getting sober for a youth pastor or to avoid some cosmic punishment, but rather because I wanted to experience for myself a fuller relationship with God. That difference—doing it not because I had to but because I wanted to—was what set me free.

Within six months of moving in with D.E., I began going to a certain 12-step program (even in print, we remain anonymous). I was twenty years old when I started, and I haven't had a drink since.

At first, I thought I would keep grace more or less to myself (apart from the occasional overenthusiastic outburst to Jesus-tattooed strangers, that is). I figured I would run a record store or open a tattoo parlor. Maybe I'd work subtle grace references into people's tattoos, as the tattoo artist had done on the ones that now covered my arms and chest. But I wouldn't make a career of it. Certainly, ministry was the last thing on my mind. I had spent my whole life trying to escape the gravitational pull of my parents' church and the endless arguments with self-righteous Christians. I wasn't about to go back.

What began to draw me out into the world, and ultimately led me back to the church, was an experience I had at a homeless ministry in Atlanta called SafeHouse. I first went there with D.E. and his church group to serve a meal. I was still pretty uncomfortable being around churchgoers, so I was reluctant to go. But then I began having these really frank and amazing conversations with the homeless people. Some of them were just plain crazy, but many of them were people like you and me who had just hit a run of bad luck or made a string of bad decisions.

Hearing about their lives and struggles put my own life in perspective. For years, I had been a one man pity-party. I felt so sorry for myself—for being a Bakker, for being dyslexic, for just being me!—that I was totally self-absorbed. I had a lifetime of excuses ready to unload on anybody who tried to hold me accountable for my own life and bad behavior. On too many occasions, I let loose that anger.

I still remember the revelation of seeing (really seeing) all the things that I took for granted on a daily basis: a plate of food, a shower, a clean room, a safe place to sleep. I began to get outside my own head and my narrow concerns, which suddenly seemed embarrassingly small in comparison to those of the homeless men at the shelter. I approached Philip Bray, who ran SafeHouse, to ask if I could work there full-time.

My experiences there taught me that I wasn't so unique and special in my misery—other people were suffering the same pain and confusion I had suffered. What's more, I realized I could help them.

I began to reconsider my decision to steer clear of Christianity. At the urging of a friend, I even began talking to groups of kids at churches and tiny concert halls. I was really nervous at first, but slowly I found my voice. I realized that I had something to say. My message was simple: "I tried to please God by living up to the rules, and you know what, I couldn't do it. But God loves me and accepts me anyway. He loves you too. Grace saved my life. It can revolutionize yours."

Still, I was scared. I knew the skepticism I would face because of my family name. (I'm still *really* uncomfortable taking part in fund-raising in any form.) What's more, I knew the opposition I would face from Christians who were deeply invested in a religion of fear, judgment, and damnation. What I couldn't imagine at the time was just how intense this opposition would be.

People Pleaser

Preaching unconditional acceptance didn't make me popular with a lot of the Christians I encountered. Weirdly, the stiffest opposition came from people at the Christian alternative music festivals I attended over a number of years. On the surface, we looked the same: tattoos, obscure punk band patches, combat boots. But the Mohawks and Misfits T-shirts couldn't hide the fact that many of these kids were deeply invested in religious law: the rules they thought determined our salvation or damnation.

I was shocked by their militancy. Booths at the concerts—even CD covers—were decorated with graphic pictures of aborted fetuses and violent condemnations of lust and promiscuous sex (to name just two hot topics). Although they had invited me to speak, when I ambled up onstage and started talking about grace, their interest turned to bafflement and finally outrage. *What do you mean, God loves everybody?!* They hurled epithets at me: "heretic," "people pleaser," and various other unprintable names. One guy even tried to fight me. Needless to say, I wasn't invited back.

I got a similar reaction (albeit less openly violent) from some of the buttoned-up Christian congregations I visited. In church we learn that we should "hate the sin but love the sinner." I was seeing Christians who were using sin as an excuse to judge and reject the people they associated with sin. Loving concern blurred too easily with scary intimidation tactics. People seemed all too eager—gleeful, even—to assign their friends and neighbors to the pit fires of hell. And they didn't care much for a young tattooed kid (let alone a son of Jim Bakker) coming to talk to them about God's unwavering acceptance. I know of at least two youth pastors who were fired for inviting me to come speak at their churches.

But as my speaking gigs took me to more places around

the country, I also witnessed the positive power of grace to transform people's lives. I watched as kids who felt damned and rejected by the churches they grew up in were renewed in their faith. That's what inspired me to start other chapters of the Revolution Church—an extension of the work that began years before in Arizona. I added chapters in Atlanta and then New York City.

Revolution started as a "scene" or "subculture ministry." We tried to restore the people who I felt were most likely to be marginalized and alienated from the church: skateboarders, goth kids, rockabillies, punks, and hippies. But I quickly realized that there was a much bigger market and a broader need for grace. I saw people from all walks of life whose relationships with God were strengthened and restored through grace. I saw the relief that comes—like a first gasp of air after nearly drowning—when people realize that they don't have to earn God's love or fear His wrath; they only have to get to know Him better.

A few years back I spoke at a big event of seven thousand Christian youth leaders in St. Louis. During the Q&A session afterward, a kid started shouting his head off in an attempt to disrupt the talk. He called me "a universalist" and said I was "preaching a false gospel." When I didn't take the bait, he ran out of the room screaming. I was shaken by it, flustered and angry and fighting back my own tears. After recovering my composure, I told the audience, "You know, that kid's passion is the kind that changes the world."

About a year later, I was at a book signing when a kid came up to me and said, "I love what you've done. Your book changed my life." I smiled and thanked him. Then he just lingered there staring at me. After a few awkward moments of this, he finally said: "I have a confession to make. I was that kid who harassed you at that event in St. Louis. But you've completely opened my eyes." I was amazed. I thanked him for having the courage to grapple with grace and urged him to pass the truth along to others.

Preaching grace opened my eyes to other kinds of suffering as well. It's what started me thinking about how Christians have mistreated the gay community, for one. I encountered numerous gay men and women who felt rejected and judged by their churches. This rejection often cost gay Christians their faith. Occasionally, it cost them their families. In some tragic instances, it even cost them their lives as intimidation—performed in the name of God—drove them to suicide. I was appalled by our behavior. Christian behavior. If grace was real, then there was no excuse for acting that way toward *any* of God's children.

But grace is bigger than any one hot-button issue. This book is about examining every aspect of our lives through the clarifying lens of grace. It applies to everything: our views of God as revealed through Christ, our image of ourselves as God's children, and our relationships to others. A deep, confident understanding of grace creates a sturdy foundation on which to build our faith, our lives, and our world. We know where we stand with God because we know that He stands by us no matter what we do.

I gained an early familiarity with the word *disgraced*. In the same way that some religious leaders are called "Reverend" or "Right Honorable" or "His Holiness," I learned that fallen preachers are called "disgraced." It's an interesting construction: *dis*-graced. It says that you were once given grace, but now you've lost it. You were graced; now you're not.

Human love is a fickle thing. We "dis-grace" all the time. We grant fame, fortune, acclaim, and attention to people (often when they don't deserve it), then we take perverse pleasure in stripping it all away. Infamy has become a kind of second act to fame in our culture. With all the tabloid scandals and mocking reality TV shows, it's almost gotten to the point where people become more famous for losing public favor—for being dis-graced—than for whatever talents or accomplishments made them famous in the first place.

But "dis-grace" has no place in our relationship with God. You won't be dis-owned or dis-avowed by God. You won't be dis-loved. You can't be un-graced. Once granted, grace is never retracted.

Too often we turn ourselves into lab rats in the way we relate to God. We expect to be shocked or rewarded by God for our good or bad behavior. But that's not God's agenda. That's not how He works. There's a powerful confidence that comes with recognizing that God doesn't dangle grace and then take it away. Grace is here to stay.

The Other Shoe

It took years for the concept of grace to really sink in for me. To this day, I am still occasionally stricken by doubt. Sometimes, when I'm lying in bed early in the morning, I get depressed and think: *Maybe I've got it all wrong. Maybe grace isn't enough.* I keep waiting for the other shoe to drop, expecting to discover that grace *is* too good to be true, that God *can't possibly* love us this much.

Like anybody else, I want validation. I want approval. I want to be told that what I'm doing is right (although I'd settle for not being called *heretic*). Whenever I walk into an arena-sized mega church or see a popular preacher on television, a little voice in my head says, *Well, this guy must be doing something right.* Then I remember that Christ never won any popularity contests. It was never about man's approval. In the words of another of my heroes, Kris Kristofferson: "You really have to get past all that—where you have enough feeling about what's right and wrong in the world to not give a shit about what kind of names anybody throws at you."[1]

I have to remind myself that my occasional doubt is nothing compared to the old terror I felt before I discovered grace. It's nothing compared to feeling judged and unwanted and hated by God. It's nothing compared to hating God back!

My life is still far from perfect. My mom recently passed away after a long, painful battle with cancer. During the same period my wife, Amanda, left me. I'd never felt so much pain before. But grace laid the groundwork for me to get through these hardships. I am able to trust and rely on Jesus. I am able to accept that pain is part of life. When I fall short, I come back to Scripture. I find a measure of peace. I try to grow little by little.

Grace taught me that I don't have to run from failure, that God hasn't abandoned me even when things get tough. I don't think you ever arrive, fully, at grace. You have to keep it front and center in your mind. You have to remind yourself every day that God's love for us is complete, irrational, and unrelenting.

After what I've seen and been through, I'm not bitter or resentful—not in my best moments, anyway. In my best moments, I'm overwhelmed by gratitude and love. I have grace to thank for that.

Part I

Revolution of God

Chapter 3

Revolutionary Road

This tyranny of the law is not permanent, but must last only until the time of grace.

—*Martin Luther, Commentary on the Epistle to the Galatians*

If you want to understand the revolutionary power of grace, how it can transform our concept of God and change the way we operate in the world, you need look no further than the example of the apostle Paul. Paul is about the unlikeliest messenger God could have chosen for grace. But precisely for that reason, he's probably the only one who could have delivered the message so forcefully.

Any recounting of Paul's life and influence must begin with the fact that he is one of the most influential—and most controversial—figures in Christianity. To some, he was a saint who pronounced the true meaning of Jesus' teaching and sacrifice. To others, he was a heretic who distorted the message of the church and challenged the religious order of his day. Maybe he was a bit of both.

Getting to Know Paul

Admittedly, it's hard to know anyone who lived two thousand years ago. Like a giant game of telephone, the facts get distorted over time—sometimes accidentally, sometimes intentionally. (Both in Paul's case.) That's why at Revolution Church I am constantly urging people, "*Read your Bible!*" I know that slogging through the Bible is a chore. (Because I'm dyslexic, I can sympathize.) But it's the only way we can begin to understand our faith, the only way we can decide for ourselves what we think and believe.[1] Otherwise, we're at the mercy of whoever shouts the loudest or who puts on the best show.

So, what *do* we know about Paul?

Paul was born to a Jewish family in the bustling port city of Tarsus in what is today eastern Turkey, which was part of the Roman Empire. Paul was himself a Roman citizen and he went by the Roman name Saul before his conversion. Saul/Paul was a tentmaker—a lucrative profession in those days. He may even have supplied shelter for the Roman armies: a major no-no if you were a Jew living under the thumb of the empire. (He must have been about as popular with his fellow Jews as a tax collector.)

Before his conversion Paul was a Pharisee, a keeper of—and in his case an enforcer of—religious law in the ancient Jewish world. Today, we often think of "Pharisee" as a bad word; the irascible Pharisees were the ones always arguing with Jesus in the Gospels. But the Pharisees were a respected sect of religious scholars and teachers, the missionaries of their day who thought that the will of God could be discerned through close reading and analysis of the Torah (or

"Teaching"), the Holy Scripture of Judaism that Christians know as the Old Testament. Paul underwent pharisaical religious training in Jerusalem, the way a rabbi would today. "I was a member of the Pharisees," he writes, "who demand the strictest obedience to the Jewish law" (Phil. 3:5).

When reading his letters, it's important to remember that there was no distinction between "Christian" and "Jew" in Paul's mind. Back then, nobody talked about "Christianity" as an independent religion. There was just a small group of Jews who saw Jesus as the Messiah heralded by Scripture, and a group of other Jews who didn't. As noted scholar Gary Wills states: "Jesus founded no new religion, and Paul preached none."[2]

In fact, Paul goes to great lengths to emphasize his Jewishness to the reader. In the Letter to the Philippians, he writes: "I was circumcised when I was eight days old, having been born into a pure-blooded Jewish family that is a branch of the tribe of Benjamin. So I was a real Jew if there ever was one!" (Phil. 3:5). He never considered himself anything else. He saw his message of grace as one that grew out of his Jewish faith.

Prior to his conversion, Paul, like many Jews, considered those who followed Jesus to be a cult built around a false messiah. In fact, Paul's particular commission—one he took to with apparent zeal—was to persecute followers of Jesus. He tried to stamp them out through intimidation and violence. By some accounts, he even tortured and killed them. That is how we first meet Paul in the book of Acts, as an official witness at the stoning of the first Christian martyr, Stephen.

Paul writes openly about his former passion for persecuting Jesus followers:

And zealous? Yes, in fact, I harshly persecuted the church. And I obeyed the Jewish law so carefully that I was never accused of any fault. (Philippians 3:6)

You know what I was like when I followed the Jewish religion—how I violently persecuted the Christians. I did my best to get rid of them. I was one of the most religious Jews of my own age, and I tried as hard as possible to follow all the old traditions of my religion. (Galatians 1:13–14)

I caused many of the believers in Jerusalem to be sent to prison. And I cast my vote against them when they were condemned to death. Many times I had them whipped in the synagogues to try to get them to curse Christ. I was so violently opposed to them that I even hounded them in distant cities of foreign lands. (Acts 26:10–11)

Why did Paul persecute Christians so ferociously? Not because he enjoyed it. Not because it gave him something to do on slow weekends in Tarsus. Paul did it because he thought that's what God wanted him to do. He thought it was what God commanded him to do. Paul's conception of God demanded it.

Still, you might question why, in light of his later conversion, Paul would be so frank about his former violence toward Christians. The answer is: because it helped him highlight the extent of the transformation that he underwent through grace.

Paul's initial opposition to Jesus certainly adds to the drama of his famous conversion story. The familiar Sunday school version of it comes from Acts, whose author liked it so much that he told it three times (in three slightly different versions). Paul (then still going by the name Saul) was walking on the road to Damascus, on his way to persecute more Christians, when Jesus appeared to him in a blinding vision:

> A brilliant light from heaven suddenly beamed down upon him! He fell to the ground and heard a voice saying to him, "Saul! Saul! Why are you persecuting me?"
>
> "Who are you, sir?" Saul asked.
>
> And the voice replied, "I am Jesus, the one you are persecuting! Now get up and go into the city, and you will be told what you are to do." (Acts 9:3–6)

In this one blinding moment everything changed for Paul: everything he understood, everything he believed, everything that drove him to persecute people. Paul realized that Jesus really was the Son of God! This encounter sent Paul's life down a completely new road, a path that would revolutionize the world.

Christ's Ambassador

As we've already noted, Paul was not one of the original twelve apostles. He didn't follow Jesus around and hear His teachings or witness His miracles firsthand. In fact, Paul never even met Jesus during Christ's earthly life. This put him outside the inner circle of the early church. Yet Paul shapes our understanding of Christianity more profoundly than any figure except Jesus. Some argue even more than the historical Jesus.

Part of Paul's persuasiveness has to be chalked up to his intensity. Paul was a street fighter, a bare-knuckle brawler who was fearless in defending his interpretation of Christ's life and death. He brought the same intensity to promoting Jesus that he once brought to prosecuting Him. And he was willing to go toe-to-toe with anyone he thought was misconstruing Christ's central message of grace, even if that someone was Peter, the "Prince of Apostles," or Jesus' own brother James. It took a lot of chutzpah to do that.

Paul was as prolific as he was passionate. Of the twenty-seven books in the New Testament, thirteen are letters attributed to Paul. (The consensus among biblical scholars is that only seven of the thirteen letters attributed to Paul are entirely authentic.[3] The other six were written—in whole or in part—by others in the style of Paul.) He is not only the most prominent voice in the New Testament, but also the first chronologically: Galatians was written around AD 50, roughly twenty years after Christ's death on the cross. By way of comparison, Mark, chronologically the first of the four Gospels that recount Christ's ministry, didn't take its final form until the late 60s AD.

Think about that for a minute...For most of the past two thousand years, Christians have assumed that Paul was writing at a greater remove from Christ than the supposed eyewitness accounts of the Gospels. Dissenters have used that fact to try to dismiss Paul. But the truth is that Paul's is the nearest record we have to Christ's life and teachings. The Gospels came *after* Paul; in fact, many scholars believe the Gospels reflect *Paul's* influence!

Paul's contribution was so fundamental to the creation of the church that one biographer concluded: "Paul, and not Jesus, was—if any one was—the 'Founder of Christianity.'"[4]

Paul was the right man at the right place at the right time for the job. He spoke Aramaic, the language of Jesus; but he also spoke Greek, the language of the empire and commerce. This is significant because it enabled him to move in circles that were inaccessible to Jesus and His immediate followers. Whereas Peter, James, and the apostles preached Jesus' message only (or mostly) to fellow Jews, Paul carried the word to the broader Roman Empire.

He would ultimately serve as Christianity's bridge between the Jewish (Aramaic) and Gentile (Greek) worlds. Some scholars believe that if it wasn't for Paul, Christianity might never have broken with its Jewish roots to become its own religion. It's in his capacity as Christ's ambassador to the Gentile world that Paul challenges the prevailing views of God and salvation.

As we'll see, his definition of grace doesn't just invalidate ancient Jewish law; it invalidates all religious law that sets itself up as a hoop we have to jump through for salvation. That's why Paul's message is so vital for modern readers. His point is that salvation is not found in any set of rules—whether chiseled in ancient stone or shouted at full volume on Christian radio. It is found in faith.

Apostle of Love

Paul's life serves as a powerful example of the transformative power of Grace. If you compare the Paul who had Christians whipped to the postconversion Paul, it's hard to recognize them as the same man. Where he once lent his boundless energy to enforcing God's law and policing the borders of His kingdom, he would later throw open the kingdom's gates to all who would enter: whether "Jew or Gentile, slave or free, male or female" (Gal. 3:28).

The same man once driven by condemnation and hatred would go on to write some of the most loving and beautiful language in the Bible. It is Paul's First Letter to the Corinthians that we most often use to express our love at weddings:

> Love is patient and kind. Love is not jealous or boastful or proud or rude. Love does not demand its own way. Love is not irritable, and it keeps no record of when it has been wronged. It is never glad about injustice but rejoices whenever the truth wins out. Love never gives up, never loses faith, is always hopeful, and endures through every circumstance... There are three things that will endure—faith, hope, and love—and the greatest of these is love. (13:4–7, 13)

The love Paul is talking about is much bigger and more encompassing than romantic love—it extends to everybody. He even puts it above faith. It's this faithful love that motivated Paul's travels and ministry. It's this enduring love that enabled Paul to push through every hardship (being stoned, shipwrecked, imprisoned) to share the good news of grace and to get people to wake up to God's hope for His people, all people.

Grace can be equally transformative for us, if we can only wrap our heads and hearts around it. The first step is to revolutionize our understanding of God. Only by seeing God through the life and lessons of Jesus, only by understanding the gift of grace—and what it says about the gift giver—can the Grace Revolution take hold in our lives.

GRACE NOTE

I HAVE A DREAM . . .

Here's the first of what I call "Grace Notes," stories submitted by people who have experienced their own trials and triumphs of grace. I think this one, from Erin of Virginia, beautifully illustrates what the Grace Revolution is all about. It shows how our concept of God—what He wants from us and for us—shapes our entire outlook on the world, in ways bad and good.

When I was eight, our Midwestern family made a life-altering, cross-country move to a gorgeous resort town nestled in the mountains of the desert Southwest. Despite our beautiful new surroundings, I was miserable. As one of the few African-American families in the entire area, our presence was not as welcome as we had hoped.

Being teased in school on a daily basis was a constant reminder that I didn't measure up, that I didn't belong. The bullying was not only allowed, but affirmed by authority figures. In one instance, I was speaking with a girl sitting beside me in class. Suddenly, I felt a white-hot shot of pain. I looked up to see the hard, gray eyes of my teacher, who was standing above me with a tightly clenched fist.

Without warning, she had hit me . . . hard . . . on the head! I burst into tears and ran out of the classroom. I hid in the bathroom until another student was sent in to retrieve me. Thoroughly embarrassed, I slunk back into the room I now hated, avoiding the probing eyes of the other children sitting at their desks. I was too afraid to tell anyone, so the teacher got away with treating me like a NOTHING. The children watched closely and followed her example.

Somewhere in the middle of this time, a distant relative came to town for a visit. She was considered "the black sheep" of her family. I could relate to that, so we soon became close. She said that she was "born again," and she led me to declare my allegiance to Jesus.

As if on fire, I ran through the wide-open door of religious fanaticism. I thought that I would find God there, but I didn't. I had faith without any knowledge of Scripture. I could not (and didn't want to) understand the dusty King James Bible that I had seen buried on our old bookcase.

My knowledge vacuum was filled not with any of the true teachings of Jesus, but with superstition and fantasies. I began to imagine things lurking in the dark corners of our house. When I had two frightening seizures, it was suggested that I must be under demonic attack. I was all too ready to believe it, so I learned what I could about binding demons and casting them to hell in Jesus' name. Before I knew it, I was pleading the "blood of Jesus" over nearly everything, trying to purge it of Satan.

Years of teenage disaster followed. I was sent to a psychiatrist who barely spoke to me, but prescribed a powerful antidepressant. On medication, I could be found at night running in circles in the backyard listening to loud music through my headphones. At times, my behavior could be completely bizarre. Once, I even briefly ran away from home. There I was, basically living in a resort community, yet spending the night on a bench! Surrounded by heaven, I was living in hell.

I couldn't maintain friendships because of my self-absorption and self-destruction. I became sexually active and it distracted me from excelling in college. To compound matters, every boyfriend that I trusted hurt me in some profound way.

* * *

As an adult, I had been "born again" ... and again, and again, and again. I kept trying to escape the failures of my past by hitting the Reset button.

Just out of college, I got pregnant and married a young man that I barely knew. We were two hurting people setting out to create a family to love.

It hasn't been easy. At the zenith of my obsession, I would awaken each morning with a new "task" to do for Jesus. I was consumed with busyness, running around doing things "for God," sacrificing more and more time and money, to the detriment of my family.

Eventually, I became resentful of the God who seemed to demand more from me than from others. I secretly wished that I was never told the "good news," so I could have mercy in my ignorance. But instead He held me to a higher standard (or so I thought). Because I "knew" what I was "supposed" to be doing for God, my punishment would be that much harsher if I did not obey as I should.

Ironically, when it seemed that I had mastered some

discipline I was focused on, I would soon "fall short" someplace else. I felt that God would not allow me to think that I could make myself into a "perfect" person.

This behavior robbed me of my peace and joy in living. Although I was young, I found myself wishing my life away, hoping that I could die early so I could maintain the facade of holiness that I was trying to project to others. After all, wasn't living according to the strict dictates of the Bible my duty as a Christian?

One cloudless afternoon, I began to contemplate throwing myself in front of a moving car while walking down the street. I knew that something had to change.

In a rare moment of clarity, I began to honestly examine my "spiritual fruit." Instead of winning converts for the kingdom of God, I was repelling people left and right. Others found me to be highly critical of any opinions or lifestyles I believed conflicted with the Bible's teaching. I was trying to manipulate God through my actions. I was desperately attempting to purchase His love through so-called "righteous acts." I was doing admittedly "good" things, but for the wrong reasons.

Unfortunately, I found myself still selfish and lacking any real love for the people and projects that I had committed myself to. So, when my circumstances did not change (including the failure to obtain that moneymaking breakthrough the televangelists spoke of), I was pissed off at God.

There, I said it . . . I was pissed!

Religion told me that I was surrounded by "sinners" who were bound for hell if they didn't repent and fall in line with current conservative Christian doctrine. If that were true, why was I the one in constant mental turmoil? As a Christian, wasn't God's love supposed to be oozing out of my pores? It sure didn't feel like it was. I had no joy or stillness within me. For some reason, the so-called "sinners" I knew had much more peace.

* * *

A dream I had a few years ago helped me to understand God's gracious love for me . . .

I dreamed that I was in heaven, being presented with a large framed collage. As I stepped closer to the piece, I saw (to my horror) that the images in the pictures represented every mean, selfish thought and action I've ever had on this earth. I saw everything that made me feel ashamed of myself, the choices I have made that caused me pain: cruelty, confusion, cowardice . . . I looked away, filled with so much shame.

At that moment, a firm voice spoke to me. I waited for the voice to condemn me. But instead, to my astonishment, the voice pronounced that the collage was beautiful! I was loved and accepted despite all the ugly things I'd done.

The dream showed me that these experiences are parts of us. I am this painful collage. I was in total shock: Despite all the mess, God is pleased with little old fractured me!

That dream still amazes me, since I've spent my whole life running away from who I truly am. Though initially difficult, I have begun to accept that God loves me unconditionally. I realize that my salvation isn't tied to the frequency and duration of my Bible reading and church attendance. I cannot give enough, nor do enough, to "pay God back." It is simply impossible.

Thanks to this revelation, I no longer condemn myself or others based upon the strict dictates of religion. I now rest in knowing that I can make good, thoughtful decisions. I pray for guidance, and trust that God will get me where I need to go.

I am still in the middle of this journey, but now I greet the future with excitement instead of dread. I'm focused on the promise of growth instead of the threat of failure.

The painful collage isn't as painful anymore. And I've started replacing the images with new ones of love and hope and, yes, grace.

—*Erin from Virginia*

Chapter 4

Bad Apples

Every sin already carries grace within it.

—*Herman Hesse,* Siddhartha

At the core of Paul's idea of grace is the belief that man is freed from religious law and reconciled with God through Jesus' life, death, and sacrifice.

We are out from under the old relationship of fearful obedience where man tries his damndest not to sin and God stands by ready to pounce when we slip up. Instead, Jesus invites us have a new relationship with God: that of sons and daughters to a loving Father.

But to comprehend what a radical idea this was in Paul's time (and is today!), we need to know a little something about the origins of Jewish law. For grace is the resolution to the founding problem of Jewish and Christian theology: that man is born into original sin.

Gardening

Genesis tells us that man once lived in a state of happy communion with God: it's the oldest story in the book—the richly metaphorical tale of Adam and Eve in Eden. In this blissed-out state of prehistory, God took care of man's every want and need. Man, we're told, knew no shame, no fear, no jealousy, no lust. We had no knowledge of good and evil. God's one rule for maintaining this fragile nirvana was that Adam and Eve not eat the fruit of the Tree of Knowledge, which of course sat at the center of Eden like a giant cookie jar begging to be raided.

You know what happens next...Egged on by Satan in the form of a snake, Adam and Eve eat the apple and they are exiled from Eden, estranged from God. They "fell from grace" and became the embarrassed, earthly, complicated creatures we see in the mirror each morning when we wake up. Or so the story goes.

Paul interprets this story literally. He teaches that because of this first mistake, the stain of sin is on all of us. It is part of our spiritual DNA, if you will: "When Adam sinned, sin entered the entire human race," Paul writes in his letter to the Romans. "Adam's sin brought death, so death spread to everyone, for everyone sinned" (Rom. 5:12).

Before you get too bummed out by this dire prognosis, we should note that Paul presents Jesus as a kind of second Adam. If the first one (Adam) introduced sin as a hereditary disease, the second one (Jesus) cures us from sin altogether. Where we get tripped up—where modern Christians continue to confuse the core message of Paul and Christ—is with what happens in between Adam's apple and redemption through Jesus.

The Law Comes to Town

The law of Moses was a direct response to our Adam condition—our corrupted nature and the fact that we kept getting caught with our hands in the cookie jar. The Old Testament story of the Ten Commandments (in Exodus and Deuteronomy) is about creating laws to protect us from ourselves, like setting strict rules (and harsh punishments) for misbehaving children.

At God's direction, Moses went up to the mountaintop at Sinai to receive the Ten Commandments along with a laundry list of rituals to practice, festivals to host, clothes to wear (God seems peculiarly obsessed with fashion), things to sacrifice, and civil laws to govern men's relationships with one another. Moses came down the mountain bearing the freshly chiseled stone tablets, which he intended to deliver to his people. But he arrived back at camp to find that the Israelites had already broken Rule #1: "Do not worship any other gods besides me." They had created a golden calf and were praying to it!

The difficulty with law, its fundamental flaw in Paul's estimation, is that it's all or nothing. You can't half-ass it. You can't pick and choose the rules you want to follow. You can't just do it *sometimes*. If you are trying to find favor with God through your actions, Paul says, "you must obey all of the regulations in the whole law of Moses" (Gal. 5:3). Either you follow the entire law or you fail the law entirely.

Sound impossible? That's because it is. Martin Luther, the sixteenth-century German monk who sparked the Protestant Reformation, learned this the hard way. In fact, it was his struggle with law that turned him into a life-long champion for grace.

Luther tried as hard as any man possibly could to live up to the law. He fasted, sometimes for three days on end. He rejected the comfort of a blanket in freezing weather. He confessed for six hours at a time, racking his brain to try to recall every sin. "I was a good monk, and I kept the rule of my order so strictly that I may say that if ever a monk got to heaven by his monkery it was I," Luther wrote. "If I had kept on any longer, I should have killed myself with vigils, prayers, reading, and other work."[1]

Despite his strenuous efforts, Luther knew he had still failed. He still fell short. After six hours of confession, he would always uncover some new sin that needed purging (and this coming from a celibate monk). His feelings of helplessness and condemnation made him desperate and angry: "I was myself more than once driven to the very abyss of despair so that I wished I had never been created," he wrote.[2] (Man, I know how he felt; maybe you do too.)

Eventually, Luther, like Paul (actually through Paul), realized that the law was rigged. He pointed to the treatment of Jesus as proof: "Christ 'committed no sin, and no deceit was found in his mouth' (1 Peter 2:22)," Luther wrote in his commentary on the Epistle to the Galatians. "Yet the law was no less cruel against this innocent, righteous, and blessed Lamb than it was against us cursed and damned sinners."[3] Though Jesus was completely innocent, the law still found Him guilty: "it accused him as a blasphemer (Matthew 26:65) and a seditious person (Luke 23:5)...The law condemned him to death, the death of the cross."[4] And if Jesus was found guilty by the law of Moses, then what chance do the rest of us have?

None whatsoever. But that's the point. By setting an impossible standard for salvation, we are condemned to fail. And when we fail, we blame and hate ourselves for it. At first, anyway. Ultimately, we turn that anger and frustration against the One who makes the rules: God.

That's just what happened to Luther. "Love God? I hated him!" he wrote of the time before he found grace.[5] This is why Paul, in Galatians, calls the law a "curse" (Gal. 3:13): It makes us despise the One we should love most. "Those who depend on the law to make them right with God are under his curse, for the Scriptures say, 'Cursed is everyone who does not observe and obey all these commands that are written in God's Book of the Law.' Consequently, it is clear that no one can ever be right with God by trying to keep the law" (Gal. 3:10–11).

Luther found the solution to his spiritual crisis in Paul's writings on grace, particularly in the books of Galatians and Romans. "God's law was given so that all people could see how sinful they were," Paul writes (Rom. 5:20). Or, as Luther put it: "The law is a minister that prepares the way for grace."[6]

When Love Comes to Town

Absent Jesus, the law would be like one of those unwinnable carnival games where you're promised a big stuffed animal if you can just throw a plastic ring over the mouth of a Coke bottle a few feet away. Seems simple, right? Only the game is rigged; the ring is too small, and you can't win no matter how many times you try!

Fortunately, Jesus offers us a way out of this ring-game of striving and failure. "Christ has rescued us from the curse pronounced by the law," proclaims Paul. "When he was hung on the cross, he took upon himself the curse for our wrongdoing" (Gal. 3:13).

With the arrival of Jesus, the law is redefined as a temporary fix: a kind of plaster cast to hold our fractured and dislocated souls in place between the injury of original sin and the healing of grace. Galatians 3:19 tells us, "This system of law was to last only until the coming of the child to whom God's promise was made." And a few verses later we read, "Now that faith in Christ has come, we no longer need the law as our guardian" (3:25).

This is the essence of grace, the point of Paul's ministry: Jesus is the resolution to the Adam problem. He is the answer to the law, its culmination and conclusion. Paul elaborates in his Letter to the Romans: "God destroyed sin's control over us by giving his Son as a sacrifice for our sins. He did this so that the requirement of the law would be fully accomplished for us who no longer follow our sinful nature but instead follow the Spirit" (8:3–4).

So what does this mean for us today? Some Christians think that we're still obligated to use the law to point out and condemn the sin we see in other people, that we're supposed to use it as a threat to drive people to Christ. I disagree. In my experience, wielding the law this way doesn't draw people to Christ, it repels them.

Paul's whole point is that we don't have to try (and fail

and try and fail, as Luther did) to meet the impossible standard of law anymore. Jesus redeemed all our failures—past, present, and future. Thanks to Him, we have a clean slate.

That's why grace is revolutionary. Instead of an unwinnable game, Christ presents us with a game we can't lose. Everybody gets the prize just for showing up. "Christ has accomplished the whole purpose of the law," Paul writes. "All who believe in him are made right with God" (Rom. 10:4). God loves us despite our shortcomings—or maybe even because of them.

The debate between law and grace is still unfolding in the church today. I would argue that it rages within each of us to some extent. As we'll see in the next chapter, it began in Paul's lifetime and it plays out in his Letter to the Galatians.

This short letter raises the most fundamental questions about our relationship to God and shapes the way we answer them to this day. What, if any, limits can be placed on grace? What does the gift of grace tell us about God? Does grace apply to people outside the boundaries of God's favored people? And most important: Is grace *really* enough to secure salvation?

Chapter 5

I Fought the Law

Nothing is so much to be feared as fear. Atheism may comparatively be popular with God himself.

—*Henry David Thoreau*

Jesus' apostles, especially Jesus' brother James, only grudgingly accepted the notion that Christ could be embraced by non-Jews. In their view, you had to pay to play. To truly follow Christ, you first had to convert to Judaism and everything that implied, including Jewish law: circumcision, eating ritually clean food, following the commandments, and so forth. These rules and ritual observances, they argued, were what God demanded in exchange for His favor.

Paul rejected this idea outright. He saw in Jesus a revolution in man's relationship with God, not merely an amendment of the old one. To his mind, the human life of God's Son, Jesus, rewrote the rules. It was a total reboot.

Paul was an energetic salesman for this vision of uncompromising grace, and his proselytizing took him all over the ancient world: Cyprus, mainland Greece, Crete, Rome, and Asia Minor (modern-day Turkey), where the region of Galatia was located. He had a particularly complicated relationship with the people of Galatia and the surrounding region. At times, it bordered on worship. When, in the nearby town of Lystra, Paul healed a man who had been crippled from birth, the townspeople mistook him for the Greek God Hermes (and his companion Barnabas for Zeus) and tried to offer him animal sacrifices (see Acts 14:8–12). At other times, the people could be murderously hostile to Paul, as when a crowd stoned him, dragged his body from the city, and left him for dead (see Acts 14:19).

His connection to Galatia was stronger than to most places he visited in part because he spent more time there. Paul was waylaid there by illness during his travels, which gave him ample time to build a relationship with the community and establish several churches of mostly Gentile Jesus followers there. He instilled in them a deep understanding of and respect for grace.

Or so he thought. Paul's Letter to the Galatians was prompted by a panicked concern that his students might be straying from the path of grace that he had set them on. His fears were well-founded. In Paul's absence, another group of religious teachers had come to town trying to convince people that grace wasn't sufficient to secure their salvation: that you needed more to receive God's blessing. Paul's letter is an impassioned plea to stay the course!

Cut Off from Christ

The debate in Galatia boiled down to a single, emotionally charged act: whether a man had to be circumcised to win God's favor.

To modern readers, this may seem like an odd proving ground for grace (even a slightly embarrassing one). But it was every bit the hot-button religious issue then that abortion or gay rights is today. Of all commandments of the law, circumcision was the most important and the hardest for the Jewish followers of Jesus to imagine giving up, for it symbolized the covenant ("sealed in the flesh") between God and the "father of faith," Abraham.

In Genesis, God is quoted as saying: "Anyone who refuses to be circumcised will be cut off from the covenant family for violating the covenant" (17:14). Some rabbinic texts go so far as to say that if Abraham had not been circumcised, heaven and earth wouldn't exist.

Circumcision represented sacrifice and adherence to God's rules, so in many ways, it was the *perfect* test for grace. Showing that even circumcision wasn't required for salvation would set a precedent for all the lesser observances as well.

Paul doesn't mince words in refuting the claim: "If you are trying to make yourselves right with God by keeping the law, you have been cut off from Christ!" he states provocatively. "You have fallen away from God's grace" (Gal. 5:4). He goes on to say: "I only wish those troublemakers who want to mutilate you by circumcision would mutilate themselves" (5:12).

These are fighting words. But his passion is justified. To Paul this isn't a matter of a single important exception to grace; it isn't even a slippery slope—it's a sheer cliff! Paul isn't rejecting just the need for a particular rite or ritual under religious law; he's rejecting the underlying principle that we can win God's approval by performing *any* action.

It's an either/or situation, and Paul felt he had to force the choice. You can't have it both ways. Either you satisfy God by following a set of rules that determine your salvation (law) *or* you are redeemed through faith in Christ (grace). If the former is true, then there was no need for Jesus to have died on the cross.

"I am not one of these who treats the grace of God as meaningless," Paul writes. "For if we could be saved by keeping the law, then there was no need for Christ to die" (Gal. 2:21). Jesus' gruesome suffering, His heroic sacrifice—if grace doesn't redeem us, then it was all for nothing.

But alternately, if grace is real, if salvation is a free gift from God made possible through Christ, then the law is null and void. Period. End of story. Any teaching that says otherwise rejects grace and makes Christ's sacrifice in vain. And that lesson applies equally to the laws of the Old Testament and to any new laws that religious leaders of today might want to impose as a requirement for salvation.

Understanding these stakes helps to explain the emotionality that courses through Paul's letter. After some perfunctory words of greeting he tears right into his readers: "I am shocked that you are turning away so soon from God, who in his love and mercy called you to share the eternal life he gives through Christ," he writes. "You are being fooled by those who twist and change the truth concerning Christ" (Gal. 1:6–7).

A little later in the letter his temper gets the better of him again: "Oh, foolish Galatians! What magician has cast an evil spell on you? For you used to see the meaning of Jesus Christ's death as clearly as though I had shown you a signboard with a picture of Christ dying on the cross" (Gal. 3:1). Paul is so baffled by their change of heart that he thinks they may be bewitched. "Have you lost your senses? . . . You have suffered so much for the Good News. Surely it was not in vain, was it? Are you now going to just throw it all away?" (3:3).

He sees the baby being thrown out with the bathwater: grace and Christ's sacrifice along with it!

Derailing Grace

Paul sets about building his case to the Galatians by referring to a meeting he had with Peter, James, and the apostles. He's trying to set a precedent by the highest authorities in the land. The meeting he references turns out to be a pivotal moment in the history and development of the church, though not necessarily in the way Paul intends. For two competing accounts of what happened at this fateful meeting result: one by Paul and another by James.

In Galatians, Paul recounts how he had traveled to Jerusalem with his followers Barnabas and Titus (a Jew and a Gentile respectively). There they were received warmly by Peter, James, and the other apostles who gave their blessing to Paul's ministry to the Gentiles. "James, Peter, and John, who were known as pillars of the church, recognized the gift God had given me, and they accepted Barnabas and me as their co-workers," he states (2:9).

Despite the warm welcome, controversy quickly ensues. "They did not even demand that my companion Titus be circumcised, though he was a Gentile," Paul recalls. "Even that question wouldn't have come up except for some so-called Christians—false ones, really—who came to spy on us and see our freedom in Christ Jesus" (Gal. 2:3–4). (You've got to wonder how they discovered that Titus wasn't circumcised. Were they literally peeping on Paul and company?) Paul continues: "They wanted to force us, like slaves, to follow their Jewish regulations. But we refused to listen to them for a single moment. We wanted to preserve the truth of the Good News for you" (2:4–5).

Paul's version of the proceedings is casual and friendly. It ends with a handshake agreement on grace. Paul, Peter, James, John, and the rest seem to agree that circumcision isn't required of Gentiles—or, by extension, of anyone else. "They encouraged us to keep preaching to the Gentiles, while they continued their work with the Jews," Paul writes. "The only thing they suggested was that we remember to help the poor, and I have certainly been eager to do that" (Gal. 2:9–10).

No rules are applied, just a simple suggestion to remember the poor. Grace prevails...for the moment, anyway.

The book of Acts tells the same story with a very different ending. Acts was written roughly thirty years after Paul's Letter to the Galatians. By this time the loose-knit Christian community had started to organize itself and put in place some formal rules and hierarchies. The version in Acts (subsequently referred to by the Roman Catholic Church as the Jerusalem "Council" or the "Apostolic Decree")[1] is much more formal, reflecting this emerging institutional structure.

Here we're told that the debate over circumcision began far away in Antioch of Syria. Paul and Barnabas were there preaching grace when a group of people arrived and argued that "unless you keep the ancient Jewish custom of circumcision taught by Moses, you cannot be saved." But "Paul and Barnabas, disagreeing with them, argued forcefully and at length," we're told (Acts 15:1–2). So far so good; this sounds like the Paul we know.

Unable to resolve the question themselves, the factions send representatives—including Paul and Barnabas—to see the church leadership in Jerusalem. Paul is "welcomed by the whole church, including the apostles and elders...But then some of the men who had been Pharisees before their conversion stood up and declared that all Gentile converts must be circumcised and be required to follow the law of Moses" (Acts 15:4–5). This is still on track with Paul's account.

It's a crucial question, so the elders go into a formal session to decide: Do Gentile followers need to be circumcised and follow the law of Moses? After much discussion, Peter, the leader of the group (as appointed by Jesus), rises and says,

> God, who knows people's hearts, confirmed that he accepts Gentiles by giving them the Holy Spirit, just as he gave [the Holy Spirit] to us. *He made no distinction between us and them,* for he also cleansed their hearts through faith. Why are you now questioning God's way by burdening the Gentile believers with a yoke that

neither we nor our ancestors were able to bear? We believe that we are all saved the same way, by the special
favor of the Lord Jesus. (Acts 15:8–11, emphasis added)

Peter comes down forcefully on the side of grace. The
"yoke" that he refers to, the one "that neither we nor our
ancestors were able to bear," is religious law; Peter rejects the
need to impose it on Gentile converts. He affirms the central lesson of Grace: that "we are all saved the same way, by
the special favor of the Lord Jesus." The debate ends there:
"There was no further discussion" (Acts 15:12).

Or does it? A funny thing happens on the way to consensus. Just as the group is breaking up, James offers a few
concluding thoughts of his own. At first, he seems to agree
with what was just said: "My judgment is that we should
stop troubling the Gentiles who turn to God..."(Acts
15:19).

But then he adds a baffling addendum: "... *except* that
we should write to them and tell them to abstain from eating
meat sacrificed to idols, from sexual immorality, and from
consuming blood or eating the meat of strangled animals.
For these laws of Moses have been preached in Jewish synagogues in every city on every Sabbath for many generations"
(Acts 15:20–21, emphasis added).

Wait a minute... What?! In one breath James accepts the
conclusion of the group that the law does not apply, that
grace has no limits. In the very next breath he reinstitutes
law through an appeal to tradition. Come again?

Tragically, this is the conclusion that gets communicated
by official letter to the Christian brothers at Antioch (see

Acts 15:28–29). It's like a rider on a bill in Congress that be-comes law: Nobody noticed it, nobody debated it, and no one intended to vote for it, but it gets passed anyway. In this case, this last-minute amendment contradicts the entire spirit of the decision made by the apostles.

Paul's version of this encounter in Galatians agrees with Peter's final remarks in Acts: Grace wins out unequivocally. But then James swoops in to replace grace with what can easily be seen as a new yoke: a set of rules supposedly backed by the Holy Spirit and the elders of the church. It's really unfortunate. This may be the moment when the grace train skips the tracks, derailing the subsequent course of the church.

Grace Plus

To this day, we continue the unfortunate tradition of carving out exceptions and making new rules that place limits on grace. Out of one side of its mouth, the church confirms God's grace and salvation through Christ alone. Out of the other side it decrees new hurdles—new laws—that we must follow to be right with God. In doing so, we act like Paul never existed. We write him out of the history of the church (or at least heavily censor him).

More disturbingly, we act like Christ never came to re-move the yoke of law from our necks and the burden of sin from our backs. By stamping some laws with the seal of God's approval (and the price of salvation), we reinforce the wrongheaded idea that we earn God's favor (or wrath) by our own actions.

I call this practice "Grace Plus." (Grace + not listening to "sinful" music = salvation. Grace + abstaining from sex = salvation. Get it, grace plus.)

Grace Plus argues that we're truly saved only if "little rules" are tagged onto the end of receiving grace. This works in subtle and dangerous ways. We don't talk about circumcision or clean foods in the church anymore, but we do make new rules, just as arbitrary, that are used to determine our damnation or salvation.

During the civil rights era (and long before), God was invoked from pulpits in the American South to warn against interracial dating and marriage. Often, Grace Plus takes more trivial forms. When my parents were growing up, secular music and dancing were considered temptations to hell. My mom couldn't go to the movies or wear makeup because they were tools of the devil. Ironically, this just makes us hungrier for these "forbidden fruits." As an adult, my mom loved to go the movies—and you all saw what happened with her and makeup.

Every generation writes their own version of this tragic equation. Religious law gets reinvented to frighten and judge anew. When I was growing up, Christians told me that the game Dungeons & Dragons was evil, the Smurfs were satanic, and Democrats were the antichrist. (I kid you not.) A friend recently recounted how his devout mother brought him a Christian audio cassette that explained the evils of "backward masking": the art of putting secret messages backward on records. According to the tape, this was the devil's way of getting into homes and taking away children's souls.

One of the artists referenced was the metal band Black Sabbath (led by Ozzy Osbourne before he became all cute and quirky). Hearing this sent my friend running out to buy all the Black Sabbath albums he could get his hands on. In fact, backward masking became so popular with music buyers that companies began manufacturing record players that played records backward with the simple flip of a switch.

More recently, children's TV characters like SpongeBob SquarePants and the Teletubby Tinky Winky have been branded as Lucifer's pied pipers for leading a generation of youth to sexual disorientation. Jerry Falwell took on the purple Teletubby with the purse in an article titled "Parents Alert: Tinky Winky Comes Out of the Closet." "He is purple—the gay-pride colour; and his antenna is shaped like a triangle—the gay-pride symbol," wrote Falwell. "As a Christian I feel that role modeling the gay lifestyle is damaging to the moral lives of children."[2]

Is there anything more ridiculous than grown men and women of God railing against toys? More important: Don't they have anything better to do?

The tradition continues among a new generation of hip young evangelical preachers like Mark Driscoll of Mars Hill Church in Seattle. He told his substantial internet following that James Cameron's movie *Avatar* was not only the highest-grossing film of all time, but also "the most demonic, satanic film I've ever seen. That any Christian could watch that without seeing the overt demonism is beyond me."[3]

Taking on such silly "villains" may serve the short-term interest of getting conservative Christians riled up and angry at pop culture and society, but it does nothing to bring people to God. Quite the contrary. Hissy-fit episodes by spokespeople for faith only reinforce stereotypes among casual believers or nonbelievers that Christianity is at best a joke and at worst an excuse for damaging witch hunts.

For many believers, it's just plain embarrassing. We want to tuck our crosses under our shirts (or cover our Jesus tattoos) so nobody associates us with those whack-jobs on TV and the internet.

Storm Warning

You see the Grace Plus philosophy rear its ugliest head when preachers like the late Jerry Falwell and Pat Robertson take it a step further and actually lay the blame for natural disasters and terrorist acts at the feet of certain liberal segments of the population that they think have failed to meet God's standards. After 9/11, Falwell went on Pat Robertson's *The 700 Club* TV program to proclaim that God had allowed "the enemies of America" to give us what we deserve.

In assigning blame, he cast a wide net: "I really believe that the pagans and the abortionists and the feminists and the gays and the lesbians who are actively trying to make that an alternative lifestyle, the ACLU, People for the American Way, all of them who try to secularize America...I point the thing in their face and say, 'You helped this happen,'" Falwell said.[4] It's the vindictive relationship all over again: When we violate God's law He punishes us, in this case by allowing planes to be flown into the World Trade Center towers.

In a 1998 broadcast of *The 700 Club*, Robertson talked

about God putting an Orlando, Florida, gay pride festival in His crosshairs. "I would warn Orlando that you're right in the way of some serious hurricanes, and I don't think I'd be waving those [gay pride] flags in God's face if I were you."[5] He did it again in 2010 with the earthquake in Haiti, which he blamed on Haitians who made "a pact with the devil" in 1804 to get out from under French colonial rule. "Ever since they have been cursed by one thing or another," he told telethon viewers on *The 700 Club* (that's right, this was all part of his "compassionate" appeal for earthquake victims).[6]

Every time I think I'm dwelling in the past or making too much of a few isolated eccentrics, I'm confronted with fresh evidence that Grace Plus is an even bigger problem than I feared. In August 2009, the Evangelical Lutheran Church of America (ELCA), the largest Lutheran denomination in the United States, voted (559 to 451) to allow gay men and lesbians in committed relationships to serve in the clergy. For many, it was a triumph of grace: an opening of the door to Christians who had committed their lives and relationships to God.

John Piper didn't see it that way. Piper is a popular Minnesota preacher and national-best-selling-author-turned-entrepreneur who has built a cottage industry (books, CDs, DVDs, websites) called Desiring God. On his blog the morning of the vote, Piper noted that at around the same time as the decision to permit gay clergy was passed, a tornado tore through downtown Minneapolis, damaging part of the convention center where the ELCA was meeting. "The tornado in Minneapolis was a gentle but firm warning to the ELCA and all of us: Turn from the approval of sin," Piper offered by way of a weather report. "Turn from the promotion of behaviors that lead to destruction."[7]

It's hard to imagine "desiring" a God who would show His displeasure by sending a tornado to do His dirty work. (With a God like that on our side, who needs enemies?) Fortunately, there's an alternative. As we'll see in the next chapter, there is a loving, accepting, revolutionary vision of God available to us, the one presented by Paul, the one presented through Jesus.

It's by getting to know Him that we complete the first step of our grace revolution: the Revolution of God.

Chapter 6

Abba

There, but for the grace of God, goes God.

—*Herman J. Mankiewicz, cowriter of* Citizen Kane

In the movie version of John Patrick Shanley's play *Doubt*, Philip Seymour Hoffman plays a Roman Catholic priest who delivers a sermon about gossip to his congregation. He tells a story about an elderly woman, a parishioner, who was spreading rumors about a man she barely knew.

She felt guilty, so she went to confession to ask for forgiveness. "Not so fast," the priest says. "I want you to go home, take a pillow up on your roof, cut it open with a knife, and return here to me." So she did, and she came back.

"Did you gut the pillow with a knife?" he asked.

"Yes, Father."

"And what was the result? What did you see?"

"Feathers," answered the woman. "Feathers everywhere, Father."

"Now, I want you to go back and gather up every last feather that flew out on the wind," the priest instructed her.

"It can't be done," the woman protests. "I don't know where they all went. The wind took them all over."

"And *that*," says the priest, "is *gossip!*"

Gossiping About God

When a Jerry Falwell says that 9/11 was a response to "abortionists and feminists," when a John Piper interprets a tornado as God's response to a denomination allowing gay clergy, this is gossiping about God. When we make up rules that have no basis in Christ's teaching, we play fast and loose with God's reputation. We insult and abuse Him by placing limits on the bigness of His love, the extent of His grace. And when our ears are filled with such gossip, it can be difficult to tell what's true from what's false anymore. We find it hard to distinguish the true teachings of Jesus and Paul from the distorted interpretations of the gossips.

We gossip about God in all sorts of ways. When we tell people that they have to wear the right clothes to church, or listen to the right music, or not see certain movies to be a good Christian, we make God petty and small. When we say that He favors one group of people over another, we make God mean and heartless. When we take it upon ourselves to use God's judgment to intimidate someone else, we abuse God's good name.

We shape our lives around this mishmash of rumors, lies, and half-truths, then we pass the distorted word along. By passing judgment we are *passing on* judgment. By condemning people, we are filling their heads with shame and guilt and puzzlement about what God truly intends for them. That's why it is so important to return to the Bible, especially to Paul, whose writings were completed at a time closest to that of Christ's own life and teaching. That's why it's so important to return to grace.

Daddy

The way to stop gossiping about God is to embrace the bigness of His love, the boundlessness of His grace. In Galatians chapter 4, Paul tells us that we are not only subjects of God, but also, via Jesus, His sons and daughters: "God sent his Son, born of a woman, subject to the law. God sent him to buy freedom for us who were slaves to the law, so that he could adopt us as his very own children" (vv. 4–5).

But what kind of family are we adopted into? How are we to relate to God? What does He expect from us? Galatians can be read as a family counseling session with Paul sitting in as therapist. He helps us get to know our sometimes distant Dad and to properly interpret His stoic silence and occasional outbursts.

Paul quotes Jesus in saying that "God has sent the Spirit of his Son into your hearts, and now you can call God your dear Father" (Gal. 4:6). The word he uses for "dear Father" here is significant. In Greek, it's *Abba*.

It's an unusual word—shocking, even. For in this one word the true nature of grace is revealed.

Abba in Greek is an endearing term for a parent. Not formal like *Father*, it's more familiar, like *Daddy*. Not:

"Father, may I please leave the table? I have finished my lima beans." More like: "Hey, Dad, let's play catch."

Abba was a buzzword long before the Swedish rock band brought it into circulation. In the ancient world, it was often a baby's first word—how a little girl or boy would say Dada or Papa: "Abba, Abba."

In choosing this word, Jesus is making the point that God is a loving, nurturing parent, not a strict and demanding master. He is inviting us to greet God with the same unquestioning love that a baby does a parent.

Evolution of God

One of the biggest challenges we face in revolutionizing our understanding of God is making sense of the competing visions of Him. There are many, and they're all backed by the same irrefutable source—the Bible.

There are Christians who make God out to be a bruising punisher: a wrathful God who enforces His demands with the kind of shock-and-awe arsenal available only to the divine. Certainly, if that's the God you're looking for, you'll find ample evidence of Him in the Bible. Fear and trembling were common themes in the Old Testament. And no wonder: God was constantly threatening to snuff out His children if they got out of line.

At Mount Sinai, when Moses told the Israelites that God was going to speak directly to them, they balked. "You tell us what God says, and we will listen," they pleaded. "But don't let God speak directly to us. If he does, we will die!" (Exod. 20:19). In Deuteronomy, He is described as "a jealous God. His anger will flare up against you and wipe you from the face of the earth" (6:15). An angel reinforces the point, warning: "Just as the LORD has destroyed other nations in your path, you also will be destroyed for not obeying the LORD your God" (8:20).

God elaborates, in vivid detail, the gruesome ways He'll punish us for failing to follow His rules:

> The LORD will send diseases among you until none of you are left...scorching heat and drought...blight and mildew...The skies above will be as unyielding as bronze, and the earth beneath will be as hard as iron. The LORD will turn your rain into sand and dust, and it will pour down from the sky until you are destroyed...The LORD will afflict you with the boils of Egypt and with tumors, scurvy and the itch, from which you cannot be cured...You will go mad because of all the tragedy around you. The LORD will cover you from head to foot with incurable boils. (Deuteronomy 28:21–24, 27, 34–35)

If the promise of favor wasn't incentive enough for good behavior, then the fear of punishment (*tumors, and scurvy, and boils, oh my!*) should be enough to keep us in line. The message of the rules was simple: Follow the law, or God will annihilate your ass.

Modern proponents of this violent vision of God will tell you that they're just keeping it real; that they're only being brave and honest in confronting the true, harsh, undeniable facts about God's nature. But by focusing only on the stories of God's angry outbursts, they *omit* more than they *admit*. Even in the Old Testament, this is a lopsided picture of God. These wrathful passages are balanced by some of the most tender and beautiful images in the whole of the Bible.

In Genesis 2, God is depicted forming man from dust with His own hands and breathing life into his nostrils (see v. 7). We see this gentle giant again in Isaiah, when God says, "I have swept away your sins like the morning mists. I have scattered your offenses like the clouds. Oh, return to me, for I have paid the price to set you free" (44:22).

So how do we make sense of these seemingly contra-dictory glimpses of God? Recent scholars including Brian D. McLaren (in *A New Kind of Christianity*) and Robert Wright (in *The Evolution of God*) have suggested that we start by plotting God's actions on a time line. When we do, we see that there's a clear evolution in our descriptions of God—a trajectory that points inexorably from judgment and punishment in the distant past through time toward for-giveness and all-encompassing love. It's not a divide between Old Testament and New, but rather a narrative that unfolds throughout the course of the Bible.

That's right: Our understanding of God (though not God Himself) changes over time. And we find the fullest ex-pression of His compassionate nature in Christ. By sending His only Son to live among us as a human, God revolution-ized His relationship with us. He showed His true nature as clearly as He could: Jesus, McLaren writes, "gives us the highest, deepest, and most mature view of the character of the living God."[1]

Literal readers of the Bible reject this claim on the stubborn grounds that *God doesn't change!* They think they're stuck with the angry God encountered in the Old Testament (and, yes, in places in the New Testament). They twist themselves into knots trying to maintain scriptural consistency.

Some red-meat Christians even want to interpret God's gift of grace through Jesus as being all about atonement—about God demanding and getting His pound of flesh. But remember, God became human in the form of Jesus. It's God up there on the cross. God is the One making the sacrifice *for us.* What could be more generous (and further from anger) than that?

For my part, I just hope God takes Jesus' advice when He says: "You have heard that the law of Moses says, 'Love your neighbor' and hate your enemy. But I say, love your enemies! Pray for those who persecute you! In that way, you will be acting as true children of your Father in heaven. For he gives his sunlight to both the evil and the good, and he sends rain on the just and on the unjust, too" (Matt. 5:43–45).

The author of the Letter to the Hebrews (who may or may not be Paul; this is one of those letters whose authorship is questioned) anticipates modern scholars such as McLaren and Wright when, in the opening, he writes, "Long ago God spoke many times and in many ways to our ancestors through the prophets. But now in these final days, he has spoken to us through his Son" (1:1–2). He continues: "The Son reflects God's own glory, and everything about him represents God exactly" (v. 3). And what does this exact representation tell us about God? That we're to see Him as an all-loving Abba, as Daddy.

Lord's Prayer

Jesus first describes God in this loving, Abba-way in the Sermon on the Mount in the Gospel of Matthew: "When you pray, don't babble on and on as people of other religions do," He says. "They think their prayers are answered only by repeating their words again and again. Don't be like them, because [Abba] knows exactly what you need even before you ask him!" (6:7–8).

He's telling us that we don't need to plead with Daddy. You're not begging for mercy, as you would with a cruel master. You don't need to impress God with the intensity of your prayers. Just talk to Him; He's listening.

Jesus goes on to give us an example of how we should talk to God in what has come to be called "the Lord's Prayer." The language isn't formal, but familiar and direct:

> Our [Abba] in heaven, may your name be honored
> May your Kingdom come soon.
> May your will be done here on earth, just as it is in heaven.
> Give us our food for today,
> and forgive us our sins, just as we have forgiven those who
>   have sinned against us.
> And don't let us yield to temptation, but deliver us from the
>   evil one.
> [For yours is the kingdom and the power and the glory for-
>   ever. Amen.] (Matt. 6:9–13)

It's a huge deal, this word *Abba*; this familiar language. It changes everything. In speaking to God this way, Jesus shows us that there is a relationship even more devout than obedience. He shows us that it's possible to know God in an intimate way, that there's a loving exchange available here. What could be holier than that?

I love the idea of Abba, because it encapsulates the fundamental change from law to grace, from judgment to love. My friend Brennan Manning wrote an entire book about the Abba concept, called *Abba's Child*. In it, he describes how transformative the Abba-son relationship has been for him: "The greatest gift I have ever received from Jesus Christ has been the Abba experience," he writes. "My dignity as Abba's child is my most coherent sense of self."[2]

I couldn't agree more. Seeing myself as Abba's son is what made faith possible for me. It was the instinctive relationship with God—dignity instead of fear—that I knew must exist, even when I was sometimes taught otherwise. I realize that this may not be so intuitive for everybody. Some of us don't have happy relationships with our earthly dads, let alone our Father in heaven. Some of us have to pay for the mistakes and failings of our fathers. But that's not what Abba demands—Abba pays for *our* failings. Every mistake you've made, every mistake you will make, Abba has paid for through *His* Son, Jesus Christ.

For me, the law was like an abusive foster dad, always beating me down. But where the law says, *You're not good enough*, Abba says, *I accept you.*

Where the law says, *Try harder. You'll never live up*, Abba says, *I have sacrificed My own Son, My own life, for you. I love you just the way you are.*

I hope you get the chance to experience God as Abba. Not with fear, but with an intimate fatherly love, because that's what Jesus meant for us. That's what He means *to* us.

Return to the Mud

Grace has given me a relationship with a loving God. And now that I have it, I can't imagine going back. But that is precisely what was happening in Galatia. That is precisely what happens to us too often today. We turn our backs on grace and return to the law. We reject Abba's open embrace in favor of a sterner, more distant, more demanding God. It's like an abusive relationship: Somehow we come to expect or excuse the harsh reaction. The alternative sounds appealing, but it can be almost impossible to break our bad habit.

Paul, understandably, is baffled by the Galatians' choice to return to law: "Now that you have found God (or should I say, now that God has found you), why do you want to go back and become slaves once more to the weak and useless spiritual powers of this world?" he asks (Gal. 4:9). Quoting from Proverbs, the apostle Peter likens this relapse to when "a dog returns to its vomit," or "a washed pig returns to the mud" (2 Pet. 2:22).

"You are trying to find favor with God by what you do or don't do on certain days or months or seasons or years," Paul explains. (Remember, through grace none of that is necessary.) "I fear for you," he continues. "I am afraid that all my hard work for you was worth nothing. Dear friends, I plead with you to live as I do in freedom from these things" (Gal. 4:10–12).

The reality is that it's hard to accept that you're accepted.

It's hard to realize that grace is enough, that God is Abba the loving Father, not a punishing deity threatening to steer a category six twister your way as punishment.

Just seeing God in the proper light isn't enough to complete the transformation grace promises. We must also come to understand ourselves properly as Abba's children. This is the next step in our Grace Revolution: the Revolution of Self.

Part II
Revolution of Self

GRACE NOTE

JESUS ♥ HOME WRECKERS

A revolution in our understanding of ourselves can be sparked by a single encounter with grace. Sometimes that's all it takes to open our eyes and change the trajectory of our lives. That's precisely what happened to Jared, the author of our next Grace Note.

•

My story isn't one that mainstream America would find "inspirational" or material for a made-for-TV movie, but the following is an account of a life full of bad decisions and the single event that changed everything...

I spent my entire life in the church. When I was born, my father was enrolled at Baptist Bible College in Springfield, Missouri, pursuing his lifelong dream of becoming a senior pastor of a church.

Even at a young age, I realized that the church rules weren't for me. I can still remember sneaking out of my room late at night to watch MTV, which was a huge no-no. I would press my ear up against the speaker of the television and watch out of the corner of my eye so as not to wake my parents up. I choked on the religious ritual that was shoved down my throat, and before long I wanted nothing to do with my father's religion... or his God.

When I was eleven, my father felt called to move the family to a little backwater town called Kingsland, Georgia. I soon discovered that the long arm of religion stretched all over creation. Along with the usual preteen confusions, I was trying to figure out this God thing. I had heard enough about Him to believe that He existed. And I had heard all about how amazing He was. But I never really saw His love play out in the lives of Christians. It just didn't add up.

I remained in that school for the next eight years, until I graduated. Along with that type of teaching came the typical rules and regulations of a strict fundamentalist church: No rock 'n' roll; it's a sin to have long hair; tattoos are the mark of the devil; rap music gets girls pregnant. The whole nine yards.

The one saving grace was that I had something of a safe haven at home. While my dad was fundamentalist, he wasn't nearly as hard on me as the school was. I wish I could say the same for the church he was leading. I clearly remember one of his deacons pulling me into a room to let me know what an embarrassment I was to my father simply because I would not fall in line.

When I was nineteen, I decided it was time for me to get out of the nest and do some living on my own. I could not figure out why living life "right" (according to the church) felt even worse than living it wrong. I jumped into living life "wrong" with both feet: alcohol, drugs, and multiple sex partners. I was responsible for breaking up two marriages as "the other guy."

Then, at age twenty-three, while living this life at full throttle, something unexpected happened: One of my sexual partners became pregnant. You have to understand that in the Deep South, this was severely frowned upon—especially for a local pastor's son.

One day, I made one of my infrequent appearances at

my parents' house. (I was probably raiding the fridge.) When I walked in, I noticed that my father had a disturbed look on his face. When I asked him what the problem was he replied with the ominous words "Let's step outside."

I was scared. Really scared. Apparently, word of the lifestyle I had been leading had reached my parents. My father was never a violent man, mind you, but knowing what I had been up to, I was terrified of what was about to come out of his mouth.

When we got outside, he turned toward me, tears visibly welling in his eyes, and he asked me flat out: "Are you doing drugs?"

I have never been a good liar, so I wasn't going to try it now. "Yes," I answered him flatly, offering no further explanation.

With that revelation hanging in the air, I decided to give him the rest of the news. "Dad, there's something else I guess I should tell you," I mumbled. "You are going to be a grandfather." I cringed at the words as they came out of my mouth. Like I said, my father is not a violent man, but if anything was going to make him fly off the handle, this was it.

That's when he said the words that changed everything for me. Wiping the tears from his cheeks, he looked straight into my eyes and said: "So, what are we going to do?"

What are *we* going to do! Not "What are you going to do?" Not "Way to screw up your life." But, "What are we going to do about it?"

He said "*we*"! We were in this together...

At that moment, in that one simple sentence, I recognized the grace of God. I finally saw, with crystal clarity, the love and forgiveness that all of those Sunday school teachers had talked about. The Bible stories and sermons suddenly clicked. This wasn't his problem. In fact, it was probably pretty humiliating for him. (Hell, it probably could have cost him his church, or at least the respect of many of his church members.) But he took it on with me.

I immediately began chasing after God...Lord knows, I had a lot of catching up to do.

That was nine years ago, and the excitement that I felt on that day hasn't diminished a bit since. I married the young lady who had my child, and today we have two beautiful sons. I became a youth pastor at my father's church so that I could share the grace I discovered that day on my parents' back porch.

I took a special interest in kids who had strayed from the straight and narrow path. I am proud to say that many a "good church family" has removed their children from my group because they "don't like the kind of kids I attract." I have seen young outcasts grow up into strong leaders.

I even started my own T-shirt company to spread the word about grace. It was inspired by a T-shirt I saw that read "Jesus loves porn stars."

Jesus loved me when I was a drug addict. He loved me when I was a home wrecker and a rotten preacher's son. I began to wonder: *Who else does Jesus love that others reject?*

My first three T-shirts read: "Jesus loves single moms"; "Jesus loves homosexuals"; and "Jesus loves smokers."

The business has infinite potential—because Jesus loves everyone.

—*Jared from Georgia*

Chapter 7

Good Sons and Prodigals

Grace is given to heal the spiritually sick, not to decorate spiritual heroes.

—*Martin Luther*

A few years ago, the Sundance Channel did a documentary about my life called *One Punk Under God: The Prodigal Son of Jim and Tammy Faye*. It wasn't the first time I'd been called a "prodigal." Nor would it be the last.

In many respects, the shoe fits. I did leave my home for years of hard living, not unlike the prodigal son in the Bible story. I also left my spiritual home: my faith and the church I grew up in. But this one-dimensional interpretation of the prodigal son tale—as a shorthand for loose living and sinfulness—misses the point of the parable told by Jesus in the Gospel of Luke. It isn't just a story about waywardness. It's about how grace goes wrong—and both the prodigal son and the good son are to blame.

In the previous section, we've seen how Paul and Jesus

revolutionized our understanding of God, who has gone from thundering Master to a loving Abba. Now, we have to undergo our own transformation: from cowering children to loved and confident children of God who can think, feel, and love for ourselves.

How we think about ourselves as God's children is a big theme in Paul's letters. Paul echoes the language of the prodigal son story in Galatians: "Now you are no longer a slave but God's own child. And since you are his child, *everything he has belongs to you*" (4:7, emphasis added).

Back to School

As you may remember from Sunday school, the story begins with the prodigal son going to ask his father for his inheritance in advance. The father, in an act of reckless generosity, gives it to him with no strings attached. So the son leaves home to go on a bender: drinking, womanizing, and partying his life away.

Then, just when he burns through all his cash, a famine falls over the land. To survive, the prodigal son ends up feeding pigs for a local farmer. He's so hungry that he wishes he could eat the pig slop himself, but even this luxury is denied him.

After suffering like this for a long time, the prodigal decides to go home. ("Even my father's hired hands live better than this," he tells himself [see Luke 15:17].) He plans to throw himself at his father's feet and beg for mercy. He even rehearses the lines he'll use when he finally confronts his dad face-to-face: "Father, I have sinned against both heaven and you, and I am no longer worthy of being called your son. Please take me on as a hired man" (15:18–19).

But his father doesn't let him beg or grovel. The prodigal doesn't even get the chance to deliver the lines he's practiced so nervously all the way home. When he appears in the distance—a scraggly, skinny, spendthrift bum stinking of swine—his dad rushes out to embrace him. The father doesn't scold him, but greets him with hugs and kisses. The father has the servants bring his best robe, some new shoes, and a fancy ring for the son's finger. He kills the fattened calf and throws a big feast to celebrate the prodigal son's return. The father doesn't want penance—he is just delighted to have his son back!

What's interesting is that the prodigal son's motivations aren't even all that pure. It's not like he's repenting out of genuine regret, having learned this profound life lesson. No, he's crawling back because he's broke. You can bet he wouldn't have come crawling back if he had succeeded or found a way to continue his life of indulgence. But the motivation behind the son's return doesn't seem to matter to the father. Seeing his son hungry and in need is reason enough to help him.

Meanwhile, the good son, the prodigal's older brother, returns from working in the field to find this big commotion at home. When he discovers what's happening—that this feast is being prepared in honor of his good-for-nothing brother—he is outraged. He can't believe the father would let the prodigal back in the house, let alone lavish him with gifts . . . better gifts than he ever got!

The good son storms in and confronts the father (my

paraphrase): "I've done everything you ever asked me and you never once rewarded me like this. It's not fair. You never threw me a big party. You never slaughtered me a fattened calf. Why are you doing this?" (see 15:29–30).

The father tries to soothe the good son's ego. "Look, dear son, you and I are very close, and everything I have is yours," he says (15:31). But he doesn't apologize for his generosity toward the prodigal son, either: "We had to celebrate this happy day," the father explains. "For your brother was dead and has come back to life! He was lost, but now he is found!" (15:32).

The point of the story is not that the prodigal son is a bad guy. The moral here is that the prodigal son and the good son both make mistakes, yet—and here's the kicker—*they're both still loved by the father.*

Sibling Rivalry

As it relates to grace, the mistake of the prodigal son is that he thinks he squandered his father's love along with his inheritance through his bad behavior. He is so broken and beaten down, so disgusted with himself for all his misdeeds and so certain of the judgment that awaits him, that he stays away from his father's house. He suffers more than necessary because he doesn't realize that the father loves him anyway, that it's impossible to lose this love. He can't fathom that he is always welcome home no matter how much he may have screwed things up.

The good son's mistake, by contrast, is that he gets so caught up in his own good works and deeds—in his self-righteousness—that he thinks he has earned his father's love and inheritance. He was doing all this "good" stuff with an agenda. He thinks that he deserves the inheritance more than his libertine brother, so he can't understand when the father welcomes the prodigal son back with open arms. "What about all my hard work? What about my loyalty and obedience? Aren't I your favorite!?" the good son asks.

The fact is, we are all prodigal sons. We all fall short. We all screw up (albeit some of us worse than others). But we compound our mistakes when we think that they somehow cost us our inheritance of grace. We get so ashamed of our failings that we don't think we can return home, when in reality God loves us no matter what.

We're all good sons, too. We think that we can earn our salvation, that we deserve it because of our good works. We're constantly seeking approval, and when we don't get it we lash out. We repeat the good son's mistakes when we think we're better in God's eyes than other people—that He somehow loves us more.

I've been on both sides of this prodigal son/good son divide. The crazy thing is that sometimes I do them both at the same time. (They're more closely tied than people think.) Our own fear of being judged causes us to judge others unfairly. We assume we'll never measure up to God's standard so we can't allow anyone else to, either.

I sometimes forget that God loves me for the mess I am, so I start seeking righteousness and merit from deeds, from speaking to large audiences or from people's attention toward me. My doubt and fear (the prodigal son side) turn to pride and ego (the good son side) when I start thinking about how many people know my name or attend my sermons (for the record, not many) or see me on TV. I get so caught up in the here and now—in my standing in God's eyes at the moment—that I forget about the fact that God cherished me before I was even born, before I did any of this: good, bad, or otherwise.

Grace offers us a way to escape being good sons or prodigals. But avoiding these traps requires a revolution of our understanding of ourselves: Paul writes that as God's Son, Jesus "would be the firstborn, with many brothers and sisters" (Rom. 8:29). What a radical notion that is...We realize we are sons and daughters of God—*siblings* to Jesus Himself (whoa!).

Being Abba's child and Jesus' sibling means getting over our inclination toward law and self-condemnation. We have to grow in faith and self-assurance, not allowing grace to be sideswiped by peer pressure and self-doubt. It isn't easy. As Paul will show us in the following chapters, even Saint Peter is susceptible to peer pressure and doubt.

Ultimately, being Abba's children means getting over our hang-ups—literally getting over ourselves. To join the family we must be *reborn* into it, as Christ was. That's what the Revolution of Self is ultimately all about.

Grace is the breadcrumb trail that leads us to God's homecoming banquet, His family reunion. The feast awaits and we're all invited: good sons and prodigals alike.

Chapter 8

Freaks and Greeks

Above all, the grace and the gifts that Christ gives to his beloved is that of overcoming self.

—*Saint Francis of Assisi*

Imagine for a minute how differently the prodigal son story would have played out if the father hadn't been there to intervene. What if instead it had been the good son who greeted the prodigal?

There would have been no happy reunion. No hugs and kisses. You can be damned sure there'd be no fattened calf or homecoming party. The good son would have lain back and watched his brother approach, his indignation growing with every approaching step.

By the time the prodigal reached the front door, the good son's anger would have been boiling over, and his first words might have been something like this: "Look at you come crawling back. Why did you even bother? You used up your share of the inheritance. And what do you have to show for it? *Nothing.* Well, don't think you can share mine. There's nothing for you here. Everything Dad left is for me. I did all the hard work while you blew it off. I earned it and you don't deserve it. Dad wanted me to have it. Now go away and don't come back...ever!"

In some ways the good son's mistake (thinking that he has earned his own salvation) is the more problematic one, because it makes it harder for the prodigal to return. Versions of this scene play out every day in real life between Christians. Half the reason people stay away from the church is because they know that the good sons and daughters are waiting at the door to judge and reject them when they try to enter.

The family counseling session that Paul began between us kids and our Father (Abba) in the previous section continues here in the Revolution of Self. Only now Paul focuses on the relationship between us and our siblings, our fellow children of Abba. He challenges us to redefine how we think about ourselves.

Paul has his work cut out for himself in this regard. You see, in his day, he wasn't just trying to reconcile a single family or a pair of estranged and warring siblings. He was trying to reconcile two cultures that were more or less completely at odds: Jews and Romans. Fortunately, he was well positioned—perhaps uniquely positioned—to attempt such a thing. Paul was able to be a bit of everything to everyone. He checked all the boxes: a Roman citizen (check); a devout Jew who had been through religious training (check); and a Christian who had the endorsement of the church founders (check).

Paul's goal was to trump the first two categories—Jews and Romans—with a third: followers of Christ. The key was to get members of both groups to think about themselves differently. Not as ethnicities or religions that were at each other's throats (to the Jews, the Romans were oppressive rulers and heathens; to the Romans, the Jews were incorrigible rebels), but rather as brothers in the same family.

Only by dropping these old, divisive self-definitions could they begin to see each other more clearly as brothers and sisters.

No Jew or Gentile

Persuading people to see themselves this way would prove especially difficult within Paul's own tradition of Judaism. Abiding by the law was what designated Jews as followers of the Jewish God and set them apart from the other tribes (and faiths) of the ancient world.

Early on, the law's strict "purity codes," as they were called, were applied only to the priestly class and temple personnel: it was how they prepared themselves to commune with God in the temple in Jerusalem. But by the fifth century BCE, as Jews found themselves exiled from their homeland and mixing more freely with other ethnic groups, the rules were extended to all practicing Jews.

"Israel must be 'holy' (*qaddash*) and 'separate' like Yahweh, so [scholars] crafted a way of life based on the principle of separation," writes Karen Armstrong in her biography *The Bible*. "The exiles must live apart from their Babylonian neighbors, observing distinctive rules of diet and cleanliness.

Then—and only then—Yahweh would live among them."[1] Living, eating, and worshipping apart from these other groups was perceived to be a precondition of God's presence—either you did so or He wouldn't show up.

Jesus instigated a radical reversal of this trend. He boiled the law down to its bare essentials, doing away with baroque ritual observances. "Do for others what you would like them to do for you. This is a summary of all that is taught in the law and the prophets," Jesus said in His Sermon on the Mount (Matt. 7:12).

With these words, Jesus opened the door for all people to seek God equally: "Everyone who asks, receives. Everyone who seeks, finds. And the door is opened to everyone who knocks" (Matt. 7:8).

Paul takes this inclusive idea and runs with it. He finds a scriptural basis for expanding the circle of God's favor in the story of Abraham, the great father figure of the Jewish, Christian, and Muslim faiths. "The Scriptures looked forward to this time when God would accept the Gentiles, too, on the basis of their faith," Paul writes to the Galatians (3:8). He quotes Genesis: "God promised this good news to Abraham long ago when he said, 'All nations will be blessed through you'" (v. 8).

Paul elaborates the idea a little later in the same letter:

You are all children of God through faith in Christ Jesus. And all who have been united with Christ in baptism have been made like him. There is no longer Jew or Gentile, slave or free, male or female. For you are all Christians—you are one in Christ Jesus. And now that you belong to Christ, you are the true children of Abraham. You are his heirs, and now all the promises God gave to him belong to you. (Galatians 3:26–29)

Paul's message—the point of his entire ministry to the Gentiles—is that you don't need to memorize elaborate Scripture or follow strict rules or be circumcised to find God. All you do is receive grace. In one fell swoop, Paul wipes away not just differences of ethnicity or religion ("no longer Jew or Gentile"), but all the categories that separate us: gender, class, status, "slave or free, male or female..." We are all one family, and everyone gets to share in God's blessing. Everyone!

Hairline Fractures

As simple as that sounds, it is really hard to accept in practice. We may recognize on an intellectual or spiritual level that everyone can share in God's grace. Yet our human natures resist this idea. We want to be somehow separate or special or different. Our egos demand it; our culture reinforces that we're all snowflakes: special and unique one-of-a-kind things. We are encouraged—by countless advertisements and self-help philosophies—to be independent, to flaunt and accentuate our differences.

When we're not busy thinking of ourselves as utterly unique, we are taught to take pride in all the things that divide us into categories, the things that help distinguish "us" from "them." At a coarse level, we separate people by economics, race, nationality, or sexual preference. Within the Christian church, we separate people by denominations, creating countless hairline fractures—lines and rules to divide us from one another. But when we play up these differences, we reinstate the law in the modern church. We redraw the lines that Jesus erased.

Growing up, I was taught that Catholics weren't going to heaven. Lutherans and Presbyterians were Catholic-lite, so we weren't sure about them, either. The Baptists thought that everyone in my parents' denomination (the Assemblies of God) were going to hell, so we thought they were too. (Fair is fair.)

There's a great episode of the TV show *South Park* that parodies this way of thinking. A group of the recently damned arrive in Hades where they are greeted by the peppy hell director for an orientation:

"For those of you who are a little confused, you are dead and this is hell," says the hell director, cheerfully brandishing his clipboard.

"Hey, wait a minute. I shouldn't be here," says one of the damned. "I was a totally strict and devout Protestant. I thought we went to heaven."

"Yes, well, I'm afraid you were wrong," says the hell director.

"I was a practicing Jehovah's Witness," protests another.

"You picked the wrong religion as well," he says.

"Well, who was right? Who gets into heaven?" they ask.

"I'm afraid it was the Mormons," says the hell director, checking his clipboard for confirmation. "Yes, '*the Mormons*' was the correct answer."[2]

Later, when Satan goes up to heaven to consult with God (who promptly declares himself a Buddhist), he finds the place empty except for a handful of Mormons playing guitar, drinking punch, and putting on plays about the evils of alcoholism.

The point is that we believers can splinter into all the denominations we want. We can pore over Scripture, finding little issues and phrases (or even differing interpretations of the same phrase) to divide us. We can each claim that our little group is the only one with a true comprehension of God's Word. We can segregate society and close our hearts because of these superficial differences. Or we can begin to patch up these fault lines and fractures we've created in the church and try to see past our differing interpretations of Scripture to recognize one another as children of the same God.

Yes, we can debate our faith—even argue. But in the end, we need to recognize that we're all members of the same big family. Faith in Christ can be the tie that brings and binds us together, even when everything else threatens to pull us apart.

Chapter 9

Saint Peter and RuPaul

Some people are so heavenly minded that they are no earthly good!

—*Oliver Wendell Holmes*

When it comes to grace, there's no room for squeamishness or compromise. Paul makes this point loud and proud in his Letter to the Galatians: You can't apply grace to other people only when it's comfortable or convenient; you can't do it just when others approve. To illustrate the point, Paul recounts a confrontation that he had with Peter about this very thing. "When Peter came to Antioch, I had to oppose him publicly," Paul writes, "speaking strongly against what he was doing, for it was very wrong" (Gal. 2:11).

Nowadays, many Christians are uncomfortable with the thought of their two most cherished saints arguing with each other. (Some believers have even tried to explain this confrontation away as a kind of staged argument meant to convey a lesson.) There's a tendency to want to think of the Christian founders as if they were perfectly formed marble statues in a cathedral, rather than living, breathing human beings who screwed up and disagreed and got on each other's nerves from time to time.

This is especially true when it comes to Peter, the "Prince of the Apostles." But Paul tells the story precisely because it's uncomfortable. He doesn't want to sweep the dispute under the rug. He wants to hold it up and shine a big fat spotlight on it. He hopes that by his example he will inspire the Galatians to stand up to the people in their midst who are pressuring them to compromise on grace as well.

The Cool Kid Table

What happened in Antioch to pit Paul against Peter? Basically, it was the ancient-world version of a high school cafeteria. "When he first arrived, [Peter] ate with the Gentile Christians, who don't bother with circumcision," Paul tells the Galatians. This is significant, because the food probably didn't meet the strict purity codes required under Jewish law, but Peter didn't seem to mind. At least not at first... All that changed with the arrival of the cool kids: the James gang. "Afterward, when some Jewish friends of James came, Peter wouldn't eat with the Gentiles anymore because he was afraid what these legalists would say" (2:12).

Paul is especially troubled by the bad example this sets for other Christians. "Then the other Jewish Christians followed Peter's hypocrisy, and even Barnabas"—Paul's old traveling companion—"was influenced to join them in their hypocrisy" (2:13). What makes Peter's behavior so unbelievable is that it's inconsistent with his own understanding of Christ's teaching. Peter says so himself in Acts, where he recounts a vision from God:

> He saw the sky open, and something like a large sheet was let down by its four corners. In the sheet were all sorts of animals, reptiles, and birds.
>
> Then a voice said to him, "Get up, Peter; kill and eat them."
>
> "Never, Lord," Peter declared. "I have never in all my life eaten anything forbidden by our Jewish laws."
>
> The voice spoke again, "If God says something is acceptable, don't say it isn't." (10:11–15)

After the vision, Peter goes on to perform another forbidden act: He enters the home of a Roman officer. "You know it is against the Jewish laws for me to come into a Gentile home like this," Peter says. "But God has shown me that I should never think of anyone as impure. So I came as soon as I was sent for" (Acts 10:28–29).

Why, then, does Peter backtrack on his own professed beliefs? Peer pressure, plain and simple.

It was fine for him to eat with the Gentiles when there was nobody there to judge him. But once James's crew shows up, Peter freaks out. He deserts his lunch mates for fear of being judged. He doesn't want to be caught dead at the outcast table!

Paul doesn't cut Peter any slack. "Why are you trying to make these Gentiles obey the Jewish laws you abandoned?" Paul asks (Gal. 2:14). "We Jewish Christians know that we become right with God, not by doing what the law commands, but by faith in Jesus Christ... For no one will ever be saved by obeying the law" (2:16). It's the same argument Paul has been making all along—only this time he's holding Peter to account.

Stand Up for Grace

So what are we to take from this story? First, that we all sometimes cave in to peer pressure. Our desire to appear good enough or righteous enough in front of other Christians can cause us to lose sight of grace and join in the condemnation game. We sometimes lack the confidence to stand up for what we really believe, so we find it easier just to go along with the crowd. (I know I have.)

But there's another, related lesson: Sometimes it takes only one person to stand up for grace. That's what Paul did with the church leaders in Jerusalem and again with Peter in Antioch. It's what he's doing here in his letter to Galatia. It takes only one person to say, *I'm not going to let Christ's love or sacrifice be distorted. I'm not going to let grace be lost.*

Sometimes, we get this mob mentality in the church where we think, *Well, if the majority thinks it is right, then it must be right. They know best.* But remember, our relationship with God isn't a popularity contest. Jesus had only twelve apostles. He wasn't crucified because a minority was against Him. He was crucified by the majority, the mob.

Christ was an equal opportunity offender. He made everybody mad because that's what it took to deliver God's true message of grace. Even His own apostles got upset with Him because of the people He reached out to and loved: sinners, prostitutes, Samaritans, Zealots, tax collectors, children (who were deemed to have little social value), you name it. He reminded the self-righteous that "healthy people don't need a doctor—sick people do" (Luke 5:31).

Too often we let fear of judgment by the good sons of the world win out over the inspiration and love of Christ. It has become such an exclusive thing to be Christian. We fear that if we show up at the wrong scenes, or socialize with the wrong people, our salvation might be called into question.

If we aren't careful, the echo chamber of our little denomination or clique can start to sound like the booming voice of God. It can drown out the real thing. If we listen too closely to human chatter around us, we can miss out on the voice of grace. We fail to share grace with people for fear of losing our seat at the popular table. Either that, or we miss out on the experience of grace ourselves because we were too afraid to venture out into the world and find it.

My Saint Peter Moment

I faced my own Saint Peter moment a few years ago when I took a trip to California to discuss the Sundance documentary. While I was in town, my wife, Amanda, and I were invited out to a drag show by RuPaul, the famous drag queen (recording artist, supermodel, VH1 talk-show host) who did the voice-over for the 2000 documentary about my mom, *The Eyes of Tammy Faye.*

Little did RuPaul realize the crisis this simple invitation

would cause me. It came at a delicate moment in my own spiritual evolution. I was working my way toward becoming a gay-affirming pastor: someone who welcomes gay people into the church without asking them to compromise their love or lifestyle. (For those readers who may wonder how this jibes with the Bible, we'll talk more about that in chapter 16.)

I hadn't yet declared this position publicly, however. And, frankly, I was really nervous about how the Christian magazines and festival organizers and even some of my Christian friends would react if they knew I'd been at a drag show.

Oh, I thought of lots of reasons not to accept the invitation. I told myself that I was trying to *gradually* bring conservative Christian audiences around to a more loving and understanding attitude toward our LGBT (lesbian, gay, bisexual, and transgender) brothers and sisters in Christ. I thought this meant not reinforcing stereotypes or inflaming fears about the gay community—and you don't get more flaming than a RuPaul drag show!

In the end, however, I decided to overcome my fears and go. When the queen of drag queens invites you to a drag show, you really don't have a choice. Thank God I went.

When we arrived at the club, RuPaul said hello and ushered us in past the crowd thronging outside. There were about ten of us in the VIP area. It was a very hip group including risqué celebrities like Dita Von Teese, the famous burlesque dancer who was married to the singer Marilyn Manson.

The first half of the show passed without incident. Then,

during intermission, I stepped outside to have a cigarette. While I was standing there, one of the drag queens—a seven-foot-tall black man in heels who was wearing a massive replica of the Eiffel Tower on his head—approached to say that he was a preacher's kid too and that he had grown up in the church. He went on to explain how much he loved my mom and how worried he was about her cancer.

"Please tell your mom that I'm praying for her and that I love her," he said, Eiffel Tower bobbing as he spoke.

"Well, let's get a picture together so I can show my mom who you are," I said, letting my guard down a little and taking a photo with him. Stubbing out my cigarette, I went back inside for the second half of the show.

Near the end of the show, a drag queen got up onstage and began spotlighting the famous people in the crowd: "Dita Von Teese is here!" (cheers). "And RuPaul is here!" (cheers). And all of a sudden he said, "Did anyone here ever watch the ministry show *Praise the Lord*?"

I thought, *Oh, no, here it comes*. But half the crowd raised their hands and cheered (and chuckled). I think they were expecting someone to come out and impersonate my mom or something. "Well, Jim and Tammy's son, Jamie, is here," the emcee said. And suddenly, this huge spotlight hit me.

As I blinked into the blinding light, the emcee asked teasingly, "Are you straight?"

"Yeah," I said, blushing and pointing a thumb at my wife, Amanda.

"Lucky girl," the emcee said. (*Right, 'cause I'm so hot. Sorry, fellas, I'm taken. Got a ring here, see.*)

And then the emcee got real serious. Standing there

in high heels and a sparkly dress, he said: "You know, this is where Jesus would be if He were alive today. Jesus hung out with the tax collectors and the prostitutes and the sinners..." He then launched into a three-minute speech about how Jesus loved everybody without judgment.

Then he looked back up at me and asked, "Jay, are you still doing your church?"

"Yeah," I answered.

"Oh, that's so wonderful, best of luck to you on that." And everybody clapped.

So there I was, stunned, not knowing what to make of this. One minute a drag queen was making cracks about whether I'm gay, and the next minute he was saying these really amazing things about Jesus and grace. I looked over at Amanda, not knowing what to expect, and she had tears in her eyes.

"This is incredible, Jay," she said. "In a roomful of people, where you don't know who believes what, they're talking about Jesus. They're talking about His love and grace and how much they appreciate the fact that you, as a preacher, are here with them, that you're willing to come out to the show and share this with them... This is where we're supposed to be," she said. "This is where God has sent us."

I realized she was right.

That night, in a burlesque club in Los Angeles, I saw people hungry for the love and truth of Christ. Not the judgment and rejection they'd experienced their whole lives in the church, but the real deal: revolutionary grace.

That's what they welcomed into their midst. That's what grace is all about: loving one another and understanding one another and sharing in Christ together, no matter who we are or what others might think about it.

No Limits

Grace crops up where you least expect it. Being at that drag show in L.A. challenged me to get outside my comfort zone. It helped me to recognize that there can be no boundaries—whether religious law or cafeteria politics or fear of judgment—on God's love.

I want to challenge everyone reading this book to push yourself in this same way. What are the boundaries you put on grace? Are there places you won't go or people you won't socialize with for fear of judgment? Maybe the judgment has to do with sexuality or drinking or different religions (or no religion at all). I'm not saying that you should do anything crazy or dangerous. But ask yourself: *What are the rules I make up about who gets to sit at Christ's table?* Then ask yourself: *Are my rules consistent with grace?*

When you see a Christian behaving in a way that doesn't conform with your understanding of the rules, do you condemn that person? Do you call into question his or her salvation? Do you say or do things to try to scare that person into toeing the line?

Are you looking out for others' best interests or are you just letting your judgment run wild? I still catch myself doing just that all the time. But it's only in catching ourselves that we can start to overcome these self-imposed limitations on our love.

We can't allow ego or fear to limit our love or compromise our practice of grace. If Paul can stand up to Peter and James, then surely we can stand up to the people who want to undermine grace in our lives and relationships.

Let grace guide you. Follow Christ with an open mind and heart. Doing so will take you where you least expect. It may even lead to the fulfillment of the Revolution of Self (our next chapter)—the death of sin and the birth of the "Risen Man."

Chapter 10

Risen Man

The man who renounces himself, comes to himself.
—*Ralph Waldo Emerson, Harvard Divinity School address*

In his commentary on Galatians, Martin Luther calls Christ "a cursed sinner."[1]

It's a provocative thing to write, and he doesn't stop there. He calls Him "the greatest transgressor, murderer, adulterer, thief, and rebel, blasphemer that ever walked among us, or could be in the world."[2]

Reading Luther's lines set off all sorts of alarm bells for the good son in me: *Wait a minute! Did he really just say what I thought he said? Christ a sinner?! I thought Christ lived the perfect life, that He was free of sin. And now you're telling me that He's not just any old sinner, but the sinner of sinners? A murderer, adulterer, thief? You've got to be kidding!*

Getting us all worked up is probably what Luther had in mind. He's trying to shock us into recognizing the revolutionary truth of salvation through Christ and the full implications it has for our lives.

When I think back to what I was taught in the church growing up, I remember hearing countless times that Christ died for our sins. But I don't think I ever really got my head around the concept. I didn't fully understand that He took on our sins; that He *became* sin so that we could be free.

But that's what Luther is saying. Anything that we might fault in ourselves, or in one another, we can now assign to Christ because He became our faults when He was crucified. "Whatever sins I, you and all of us have done, or will do later, are Christ's own sins," writes Luther, "as truly as if he himself had done them."[3]

All-Time Quarterback

Unburdening ourselves of sin in this way is essential to completing the Revolution of Self. We have already revolutionized our conception of God (going from damning deity to loving Abba). We have already seen that the "yoke" of law no longer applies, thanks to grace. But we don't really get over ourselves until we can get over our sin. We need to really commit to giving all of our mistakes (our sins) as well as all the credit (for our salvation) to Jesus. It's the only way that grace works.

The first step is respecting what Christ actually accomplished on the cross. There's a temptation to only half-commit to the idea of salvation through His sacrifice. We want to think that Jesus died just to help us follow the law of God a little bit better. At the end of the day, we want to take some measure of credit for our 100-yard drive to salvation. We want to be the stars of our own Super Bowl Sunday. Sure, maybe we'll say "all glory to God" in our postgame interview. But only after we've spiked the ball, slapped a few hands, and watched our righteous moves play back on the Jumbotron.

But as Paul reminds us, that's not how grace works. God has redeemed us "through Christ Jesus, who has freed us by taking away our sins" (Rom. 3:24). We don't deserve grace and we didn't earn it. "Can we boast, then, that we have done anything to be accepted by God?" Paul asks. "No, because our acquittal is not based on our good deeds. It is based on our faith. So we are made right with God through faith and not by obeying the law" (3:27–28).

The very idea of accomplishing our salvation contradicts grace. If you've already received salvation through your faith, then you can't earn it by your actions. "We all can be saved in this same way, no matter who we are or what we have done," Paul writes in Romans. "For all have sinned; all fall short of God's glorious standard. Yet now God in his gracious kindness declares us not guilty" (3:22–24).

Taking any degree of credit ourselves reduces Jesus to little more than a cheerleader, encouraging us on to the end zone. The fact is, we owe it all to Jesus. He accomplished it all by Himself. He's the All-Time Quarterback, as well as the defensive line, the running back, the tail end...

We're not even the wide receivers standing in the end zone ready to catch His Hail Mary pass of grace.

If you want to find a place in this tangle of sports metaphors, think of yourself as the die-hard fan who gets to share in the glory of Christ's victory over sin—even though you didn't do a thing to accomplish it. We all just sat there on our barstools and watched it happen. We don't share the credit, just the reward. But it's enough to set us free.

If Jesus takes away our sins, then we are relieved of them. We can start to think of ourselves not as born losers saddled with Adam's original mistake, but as part of a winning team. It's like T-ball: Everybody gets a trophy just for showing up.

Missing the Mark

So what does this mean? Are we still sinners? Well, yes. Sort of.

Paul reminds us that no one is perfect or blameless: "All have sinned; all fall short of God's glorious standard" (Rom. 3:23). He's especially hard on the sinner he knows best: himself. "I know I am rotten through and through so far as my old sinful nature is concerned," he says in Romans (7:18).

So it's not as if, due to grace, we suddenly don't sin anymore. Rather, the whole nature of the crime has changed. And, more important, so has the punishment. Through Christ, God forgives us for all the sins we have committed. He forgives the sins we will commit in the future. He knows we're hardwired to fall short, yet He announces that He loves us despite all that.

Reading Paul, we begin to get a clear sense of what sin *is not*. Sin *is not* an insurmountable hurdle to salvation (which, we already know, is achieved only through faith). Sin *is not* a hellfire offense punishable by eternal damnation. (Christ took care of that for us.) Okay, you ask, then what the hell *is* sin?

Sin is what separates us from God and the revolutionary promise of His grace. The Greek word for sin (*hamartia*) literally means "to miss the mark"[4] When we commit some selfish or hurtful act, when we lie or cheat or steal or covet, we miss the mark. And when we miss the mark, we miss out on the potential of a new grace-filled life through God.

Sin is still "bad," mind you. But it is bad *for us.* Abba isn't mad at us for our sin. If anything, He probably feels sorry for us because He knows it prevents us from fulfilling our potential. Sin carries its own punishments: It prevents us from completing the radical transformation that God intends. It prevents us from realizing God's grace.

Does this mean that God stops loving us when we sin? No! Absolutely not. Nothing can ever get in the way of that. Paul goes overboard to make that point:

> I am convinced that nothing can ever separate us from his love. Death can't, and life can't. The angels can't, and the demons can't. Our fears for today, our worries about tomorrow, and even the powers of hell can't keep God's love away. Whether we are high above the sky or in the deepest ocean, nothing in all creation will ever be able to separate us from the love of God that is revealed in Christ Jesus our Lord. (Romans 8:38–39)

Grace Bubble

The Revolution of Self culminates in a mind-bending personal transformation, one that metaphorically parallels Christ's own death and resurrection.

Paul states it beautifully in Galatians: "Those who belong to Christ Jesus have nailed the passions and desires of their sinful nature to his cross and crucified them there" (5:24). Just as Jesus died and rose again to take His place beside God, we are invited to die to ourselves and be reborn in Christ. "I died to the law so that I might live for God. I have been crucified with Christ," Paul explains by way of example (Gal. 2:19). "I myself no longer live, but Christ lives in me" (2:20).

Ours is not a physical death and resurrection, mind you, but a spiritual one. Paul says, "We died and were buried with Christ by baptism. And just as Christ was raised from the dead by the glorious power of the Father, now we also may live new lives" (Rom. 6:4). It is a total redo: You die and you are born anew. You throw out the old messy you and start from scratch. Are you ready for that?

The only way to live out the "new lives" that Paul describes is to shed our old selves. We need to check our bodies at the door. As Paul says: "I myself no longer live, but Christ lives in me" (Gal. 2:20). But what does this mean, exactly? By "dying to our flesh," Paul doesn't mean that we no longer experience bodily pleasures. We don't become some kind of skin-and-bones ascetics in loincloths, or automatons who never enjoy a good meal or have sex. No, the "flesh" he refers to is our pride and ego, the part of ourselves that constantly wants credit. Our flesh is our selfish side, the voice in our heads that says it's all about *I, me, mine*—that it's all about our wants and desires to the exclusion of everyone else's.

Pursuing our selfish flesh ultimately leads to disappointment. Physical pleasures are fleeting and insatiable—we can't ever get enough. And the more we build up our egos on the opinions of others, the harder we fall when they inevitably disapprove of us.

What's interesting is that the cost of rebirth—losing your ego, giving up your selfish pursuit of pleasure and glory—is really no cost at all. It's a burden lifted, a relief. On the other side of rebirth, you come to see that all the stuff you were so attached to before was really just bogging you down.

Grace empowers you to escape all that. "If your sinful nature controls your mind, there is death," Paul advises. "But if the Holy Spirit controls your mind, there is life and peace" (Rom. 8:6). You are free!

Our priorities are reoriented in such a way that we think about what is selfless and holy. We are overcome by the generosity of God's gift of grace. We are inspired to be more grateful and generous in our own lives toward all those we encounter.

This is what I always imagine when I see Renaissance paintings of Jesus and the saints. You know, the ones where they have those golden disks behind their heads. That is the Holy Spirit operating through them. They're walking around in a kind of "grace bubble," in a constant state of communion with God. Everything they do is a blessing. Everything they say is a prayer.

Body of Christ

Having shed our old bodies, Paul tells us, we are born into a new one: "one body in Christ" (Rom. 12:5). We become new people, "risen men"—with Christ living in and through us.

What does a risen man look like? Well, Paul is a pretty good example. We see the Holy Spirit acting through him in his most moving and beautiful passages: "Since God chose you to be the holy people whom he loves, you must clothe yourselves with tenderhearted mercy, kindness, humility, gentleness, and patience. You must make allowance for each other's faults and forgive the person who offends you," he writes in his Letter to the Colossians (3:12–13). "Remember, the Lord forgave you, so you must forgive others. And the most important piece of clothing you must wear is love. Love is what binds us all together in perfect harmony" (vv. 14–15).

The risen man is someone who is wholly transformed—holy and transformed. As we'll see in the next section (Revolution of Society), the risen man operates in an entirely new way in the world. Grace transforms his personal relationships and his commitment to fellow human beings. It inspires him to change the world, not because he's trying to earn his way into heaven, but because he genuinely cares about others.

God Is My Designated Driver

When I think about the awesome gift of grace, of God's unwavering love for us, I'm encouraged to rethink myself. I'm not a good son or a prodigal anymore, but a true son of Abba, a sibling to Jesus. Paul is an inspiration to me. I want to experience the all-encompassing love that he describes.

But I have an awfully long way to go. The first step, for me, has been to trust God a little more. "If we are living now by the Holy Spirit, let us follow the Holy Spirit's leading in every part of our lives," Paul advises (Gal. 5:25).

Choosing grace has meant turning the keys to my life over to the Holy Spirit. For too long, I had been driving drunk on my own ego and striving and selfish desires. But lately I've stopped trying to dictate every outcome in life. I've realized I can't always make the world conform to my wishes. Grace means letting go and letting God take the wheel.

In tough situations, when I get angry or frustrated with friends or people I encounter in the church, I have to step back and decide, *Okay, I'm not going to demand my own way in this situation. I'm going to be patient, because I think that there might be a better way to deal with this. I'm going to give God time to work it out and show me the right way to handle this situation.*

And you know what? It works. God wants what's best for us. He wants us to experience peace and patience. If we let Him, He will help us discover joy and comfort in our lives, even when we're going over a rough patch. (Maybe not always on our schedule, but eventually God does.) I'm beginning to find a measure of those qualities through grace.

I want to challenge you to do the same. Try observing your motivations for a day. Maybe keep a journal and check in on yourself every few hours. Are you thinking about yourself or others? Have you done something harmful or dishonest, no matter how small? If not, check back in another hour...Just wait, you will. We all do.

When you do something selfish, when you miss the mark, don't beat yourself up over it. But do pay attention: I'll bet that if you really probe your motivations, you'll find that you were thinking about yourself when you did it. What you soon realize is that all our anger and resentment and jealousy and greed comes from thinking about Numero Uno, that's right, ourselves.

The good news is that the opposite is also true. Check in on how you feel when you do something truly generous. Pay close attention at first, because you may find that a lot of what you "do for others" is really about yourself. But if you watch your motivation, you'll see a big difference between selfish acts and genuine caring. Genuine caring is much more gratifying because it connects us to one another.

The next time you're in a crowded subway or a mall, look around at people. Try for a moment not to see them as separate, as something that stands between you and your next destination or satisfying your next desire. Rather, think of yourself as part of the same body, Christ's body. Imagine their pain as your pain. Imagine their joy as your joy.

How does seeing people this way change your outlook? Through grace, through faith in Christ and an overwhelming sense of gratitude for God's love for us, we can do it. Try to "die to yourself" for a day, an hour, even sixty seconds—you won't be disappointed. Now imagine living every moment of your new life this way. That is what Jesus challenges us to do. As grace grows in our lives, that is what God inspires us to do.

In the next section, the Revolution of Society, we'll

wrestle with the question of motivation. At first, it may seem "easier" to do what is good when there is a punishment or reward to motivate you. (This is the underlying principle of law.) But Paul shows us a powerful alternative—a *freedom* to do good—through grace.

Part III

Revolution of Society

GRACE NOTE

COMING AROUND ON GRACE

This story from Dale in Arkansas is a great setup for the Revolution of Society, because it demonstrates how grace can operate quietly in the background of our lives to change our relationships and, ultimately, our world.

I grew up in a very strict Holiness Pentecostal home. I was raised in a church (and home) where my brothers and sisters were not only taught right from wrong . . . it was drilled into our brains. Still, my family and I were always very, very close.

As I got older, I started to have thoughts and feelings that I was somehow different. My brothers would talk about girls. My sisters would talk about the guys that liked them. Me, I would think about the guys that liked my sisters . . . *How funny!*

Growing up, my father was also my pastor. One *big huge* sin according to Pentecostal doctrine is homosexuality. When I was around fourteen or fifteen years old, I finally came to terms with what I was feeling inside and what it really meant. It shocked the hell out of me.

Or, rather, it shocked the hell into me: Given what we'd been taught, how could I ever tell my family and my friends? What would everyone think of me? Would the family that I was so close to and loved so dearly leave me out in the cold?

I decided that the safest course was to keep my secret to myself. I didn't say a word to anyone. But I guess my family could "just tell."

Each Sunday morning, my older brother would stand in front of the pulpit of our beautiful church (which I decorated) and welcome our father and hand him the morning sermon. But, little by little, the sermons began to change. They were less about hellfire and brimstone anymore. They were delivered with more love and caring.

Church wasn't the only place I noticed the change. At night, I would see my dad upstairs in his home office studying like an honor roll student cramming for finals. He would have every Bible out that you can imagine, every Bible dictionary he could get his hands on, along with notebooks full of notes...

Even though my secret was unspoken, he was clearly searching his faith for answers. From that point forward, he never preached against homosexuality again. I'm sure I'm not the only one who noticed the conspicuous absence of this hot topic.

When I was twenty-two years old, in college, I got a call from my sister. She said, "Meet me at the river, we need to talk." *Oh my God*, I thought, this was going to be it. This was the day I was finally going to tell a family member who I was. I *had* to get it out...

That afternoon, my sister and I had a long heartfelt discussion. We cried and laughed. It was the closest I ever came to feeling "born again." She also broke the news that my mother knew. (Of course! Moms always know everything.)

A few months later, I packed up the car and went back home for the weekend. I walked in the house, and to my surprise it was very quiet. You see, my parents had eleven children, so it was *never* quiet. This was one of those rare days that my mother had the house to herself.

I walked in the kitchen and she was baking me a cake. This was the day that my mom and I "talked."

"I have something to say to you," she began. "I know that you have started to tell people something that is important to you. After years of talking about this with your father, we want you to know that we love you, we care about you, and we want you to be happy.

"We want to be part of your life with whomever you choose," she continued. "After all, how can we as Christians stand before a crowd and teach God's grace and love each Sunday if we can't live it in our own lives?"

This meant the world to me. For years I had guarded my secret because I was scared that I would lose the love of my family. And here they were reaching out to me, telling me I was still loved and cared for and that their only wish was for me to be happy. It was literally the happiest day of my life.

One year from the day of my talk with my mom, my parents surprised me again by introducing me to someone. We went out on one date, and I knew this one was special...I mean come on, he already knew my parents!

What an awesome man he was. We spent six truly wonderful years together before he died in a car accident in June 2005. It has been rough going through life without him, but he also taught me a lot about love and grace. I take his memory with me everywhere I go!

So many times we hide from the truth for fear of what others will see us as or what they will think of us. But God's grace and His love have taught us something different.

What a feeling to have—that even when the "world" shuns us, the love and grace of our God is there for us. It can even, slowly, bring the world around to loving us too.

—*Dale from Arkansas*

Chapter 11

The Fruit

In the New Testament, religion is grace and ethics is gratitude.
—*Thomas Erskine, Scottish theologian*

Whenever I preach about grace, I get the same question: "What about 'faith without works is dead'?"

It's a quote from James—yes, the same guy Paul tangled with over grace in Antioch back in chapter 5. "Suppose you see a brother or sister who needs food or clothing, and you say, 'Well, good-bye and God bless you; stay warm and eat well'—but then you don't give that person any food or clothing. What good does that do?" James asks (James 2:15–16). "So you see, it isn't enough just to have faith. Faith that doesn't show itself by good deeds is no faith at all—it is dead and useless" (v. 17).

The idea of doing "good works" is attractive to many of us. After all, Jesus fed the hungry, didn't He? He attended the sick and healed the lame. He even raised the dead. At a fundamental level, we want to see our faith impact and improve the world in some way. We want *being* good to translate, on some level, to *doing* good.

The good news is that it can. But the only way to do it honestly and sustainably (and unselfishly) is through grace. We have already seen how grace transforms our perception of God and emancipates us from the shackles of law. We have seen how, freed from our sin-nature, we think about ourselves differently and are born anew. Now we need to apply the lessons of grace to revolutionize our relationships in the world around us.

Keeping Up with the Jameses

The first step is to realize that if law is no longer the means to salvation, that applies to both good and bad actions alike. "Works" include *any* action we think we have to do (or avoid) to earn God's blessing and our own salvation.

The problem with "works" is that they ultimately don't work. The name says it all. We *work* so we can *earn* salvation. Like a wage. But as we've seen, the pay stinks. It's literally slave wages. No matter how much we do and earn, no matter how hard we try, it's never enough to buy the one thing we really want: which is to please God and be united with Him.

This doesn't mean that we shouldn't do good deeds in the world. In fact, as we'll see, grace can empower us to do far more good for others than even religious law requires.

It all comes down to motivation. James writes: "I can't see your faith if you don't have good deeds, but I will show you my faith through my good deeds" (2:18). This is not to cast James in the role of villain. He is concerned about what might be called "cheap grace" or "dead faith"—people who use grace as an excuse to ignore the people around them. The problem with the way James expresses it is that "works" can too easily slip back into law. It can feel like we need to see—and show—our faith through deeds to meet God's standard.

The trouble is, if everything you do comes back to your own personal cosmic scorecard, you're not really caring about others. Your selflessness ends up being self-obsessed. *You* are all that you think about. Where's the generosity in that?

When you try to earn salvation through works, you judge your neighbor by the same harsh standard that you use to judge yourself. Instead of being encouraged by other people's good deeds and generosity, you fall into a pointless competition, trying to do a little better and be a little more virtuous than your neighbor. You are keeping up with the Jameses.

To avoid this trap, we have to find a motivation that lies outside law and works. We have to find a source of inspiration beyond obligation or pride. We find it in the freedom of grace. But free isn't easy . . .

Nothing Left to Lose

"Christ has really set us free," Paul declares triumphantly near the end of his Letter to the Galatians (5:1). Freedom from law is the overarching message of this letter—of his entire ministry, you might say. It is the essence of grace.

All right, we're free. So now what? Free *to do* what?

By definition, freedom makes room for mistakes. We have the freedom to do good, yes. But we also have the freedom to screw up royally. Or to do nothing at all. That is the price of being free. It's up to us.

Paul describes two paths of freedom that we can choose to pursue. The first is a base sort of freedom that involves indulging our sinful natures without repercussions (at least as far as God's punishment is concerned). The second is a higher, grace-inspired form of freedom that gives us direction and motivation to do good in the world.

It's clear which one he recommends. "You, dear friends, have been called to live in freedom—not freedom to satisfy your sinful nature, but freedom to serve one another in love," Paul writes (Gal. 5:13). "So I advise you to live according to your new life in the Holy Spirit. Then you won't be doing what your sinful nature craves" (5:16).

The contrast between these two freedoms is as stark as can be. You might say they represent Paul's vision of hell and heaven—but both play out here on earth.

First, let's look at the hell scenario.

What happens when we exercise our freedom to sin? Paul rattles off a long dirty-laundry list of unhappy results:

When you follow the desires of your sinful nature, your lives will produce these evil results: sexual immorality, impure thoughts, eagerness for lustful pleasure, idolatry, participation in demonic activities, hostility, quarreling, jealousy, outbursts of anger, selfish ambition, divisions, the feeling that everyone is wrong except those in your own little group, envy, drunkenness, wild parties, and other kinds of sin. (Galatians 5:19–21)[1]

Some of the concepts sound antiquated and preachy in tone: "eagerness for lustful pleasure, idolatry, participation in demonic activities..." But others hit close to home: "hostility, quarreling, jealousy, outbursts of anger, selfish ambition,...envy, drunkenness, wild parties..." (Been there, done that.) I especially like that Paul includes "the feeling that everyone is wrong except those in your own little group." He is speaking directly to the good son in each of us, addressing the small-mindedness and false divisions we create in the Christian church today.

We all struggle to some degree with the temptation to pursue the "sinful" path of freedom. And because Jesus redeemed us from law, we have the "freedom" to indulge these desires if we want to. It won't cost us God's love. Paul ends this verse (5:21) saying, "Let me tell you again, as I have before, that anyone living that sort of life will not inherit the Kingdom of God." By this he doesn't mean that they determine our salvation—he's made it abundantly clear that no deeds can. By "Kingdom of God" he means a more earthly communion with God. (More on the "Kingdom of God" in chapter 13.) But make no mistake, these are bitter, bitter fruits. They will enslave you.

The freedom to indulge our sinful side is not a very satisfying freedom at all. It's basically the freedom to screw up our lives and hurt those around us. This is the notion of sin that we were introduced to back in chapter 10 of this book: mistakes that carry their own punishment. When you are reckless with your freedom, you end up hurting yourself.

Fruit of the Spirit

Contrast this with Paul's positive vision of freedom: "When the Holy Spirit controls our lives, he will produce this kind of fruit in us: love, joy, peace, patience, kindness, goodness, faithfulness, gentleness, and self-control" (Gal. 5:22–23).

These "fruit of the Spirit," as they are called, are the payoff of grace. Where we were once ensnared in sin by a single apple, now, through grace, we produce a virtual cornucopia of positive fruit. The fruit of the Spirit are holy concepts, relief words. Take a moment to reflect on each of them...

Love
Joy
Peace
Patience
Kindness
Goodness
Faithfulness
Gentleness
Self-control

If you rushed over them, go back and read each one slowly. Get a feel for these words. Are they familiar? I bet they are—so much so that we don't even need to define them; we know exactly what they mean, though we don't spend nearly enough time savoring them in our lives.

The fruit of the Spirit are the best of our selves: God acting in and through us. Look at the list again. Is there any fruit that you'd throw out? "Self-control," maybe. It sounds a little cranky and bossy; a little too close to law, right? But it is only through self-control that we can exercise the other fruit. Self-control is what saves us from our own recklessness, our own inclination to use our freedom to destructive ends.

Imagine life as an exercise in the fruit of the Spirit. Imagine being filled with them 24-7. How do they make you feel? Happy? Relaxed? Satisfied? Refreshed? Isn't it a "freer" kind of freedom than the alternative described above?

Unfortunately, in our ignorance, we too often choose the lower, fermented fruit over the fruit of the Spirit. Sometimes we do it unconsciously. We opt for jealousy over joy, lust over love, outbursts of anger over patience. We think that these selfish fruit will make us happier—and they may, in an instant-gratification, short-term way. But not over the long run.

One of the things I learned in a 12-step program was to "think through a drink." You imagine that you've had the drink you so desperately want and you think about how you'll feel on the other side. You anticipate the cost and you ask yourself: *Is this one moment of escapism going to be worth the reality I'll face when it's over?* We can do that with every temptation in our lives. We can think through a lust, think through an angry outburst. We can think through a fit of misdirected pride. The reality is, once you've taken their full measure, none of these temptations look very appealing on the other side.

In the long run, these actions don't enrich your life or strengthen your relationships. They don't make you a better friend, a better child, a better parent, a better lover. Thinking selfishly for a moment, they don't even make you any more fulfilled.

Ultimately, the fruit aren't about us at all. A tree doesn't eat its own fruit. The fruit is supposed to be picked and enjoyed by other people. Sometimes it's hard to put other people first, but that's what we're called to do. God gives us His love so that we can love others.

Our fruit say a lot about us. In the Gospel of Matthew, Jesus says: "A healthy tree produces good fruit, and an unhealthy tree produces bad fruit... The way to identify a tree or a person is by the kind of fruit that is produced" (7:17, 20). In other words, a person living a life of grace and inspiration will be loving, joyful, peaceful, patient, kind, good, faithful, gentle, and in control.

You're not always going to be perfect. There are bound to be a few sour apples on your tree. But if you stick with grace, the fruit of the Spirit will grow over time. For some, it may happen quickly; for others, it could take quite awhile. But when you're responding to life out of love and not fear, the fruit of the Spirit will ripen in your life.

People who choose to exercise their sinful freedoms, on the other hand, will see the fruit replaced by the thorns and thistles of anger, jealousy, and selfish ambition.

How do you want to fill your plate?

The James Gang

Grace is not about showing *others* what you do. It's not even about showing God what you do. It's about *seeing* God for who He is (a loving Father), and being changed by that encounter.

It's when we manage to forget about ourselves that we

can truly focus on Christ and let go of our selfish interests. The path of believing that our salvation depends on works, even good works, destroys our love of God. This means-to-an-end relationship with God is a dead end. The path of faith and fruit, by contrast, makes all good works possible. It is the difference between obedience and gratitude.

Works says: Be good, or else...

Grace says: Be grateful, and then...

Getting back to James's original example, we don't "demonstrate" our righteousness by feeding the homeless and hungry person; we celebrate our freedom by doing so. We do it because we care—genuinely and deeply—for the welfare of others.

Try it out. Do something generous this week that you decide never to tell anyone about: not your best friend, not your spouse, not your parents. Just you. It can be small, but it will be yours. See how it makes you feel. I'll bet it will feel good. Even better than doing something for yourself.

These are the fruit of grace.

Chapter 12

Clint Eastwood Jesus

Conventional wisdom holds that if your faith can survive your filled-with-angst teenage years and troubled twenties, then it is secure. You're a lifer. But more and more, I'm seeing the opposite: Lifelong Christians are losing their faith when they reach maturity.

It's not that they've lost their love for God or their belief in Jesus, necessarily. Rather, they're driven away from the church—and sometimes even their private faith—by the behavior of their fellow Christians.

Paul saw the train wreck that awaited the church if we got grace wrong. That's why, as he nears the end of his Letter to the Galatians, he focuses on one gracious act, one fruit in particular: restoration.

He begins the discussion in Galatians 5 with a warning:

"If instead of showing love among yourselves you are always biting and devouring one another, watch out! Beware of destroying one another" (v. 15). It's love on the one side, destruction on the other.

He picks up the theme again a few verses later. "Dear friends, if a Christian is overcome by some sin, you who are godly should gently and humbly help that person back onto the right path," he writes. "And be careful not to fall into the same temptation yourself" (Gal. 6:1).

The definition of *restoration* is the return of something to its "former, original, or unimpaired condition."[1] The word always reminds me of classic cars. I remember going to Pigeon Forge, Tennessee, once to see a muscle car show of vintage Cadillacs and Chevys. Here were all these beautiful cars from the 1930s and 1940s that had been so well restored that they looked like they'd never left the sales lot. They had perfect chrome and unblemished paint jobs on the outside. And when you looked inside, you realized that they had state-of-the-art sound systems and all these modern electronics. They were actually better than new!

In the Christian context, restoration means helping people who falter. Instead of condemning and rejecting them—consigning them to the spiritual junkyard—we restore them. It means saying: "Okay, you've screwed up, but God hasn't given up on you."

It's not even about restoring them to God's love; it's about reminding them that God's love can't be lost in the first place.

In the Gospel of Matthew, Peter comes to Jesus and asks, "'Lord, how often should I forgive someone who sins against me? Seven times?' 'No!' Jesus replied, 'seventy times seven!'" (18:21–22). He is telling us that, practically speaking, we shouldn't place any limits on our willingness to forgive and restore other people.

This is where our human limitations become apparent. Restoration can be a painstaking process; it can take a long time. Sometimes we just aren't up to it. We also have to be smart about *how* we restore. Blind restoration can be unwise, even foolish. Consider the extreme case of a serial rapist or a child molester. Restoration doesn't mean acting as though these things never happened. It certainly doesn't mean placing people back in a situation where they're going to be tempted to do harm to themselves or others. (You don't invite an alcoholic to bartend.) But God's unconditional love is an example to us that we should do everything in our power to restore people. We must find the generosity, the patience, the strength to act out of love and give people the help they need to recover. We need to provide them the tools to rebuild their lives.

It's because someone restored me that I came back to faith and ministry. My friend D.E. stood by me and tolerated me even when I was calling him a heretic and a sellout, even when I was drunk all the time. Eventually, his persistence paid off.

We have to remind one another of the freedom to fail. If we thought that we could be transparent about our shortcomings and our doubts without being destroyed, then we might be willing to air our problems sooner. We might feel secure enough to seek help when our problems are still small and manageable, before they consume our whole lives.

Compassion Play

The classic story of restoration in the Bible is the allegory of the adulteress from the Gospel of John. By this point in Jesus' short life, He has already made quite a name for Himself. He has been running around performing miracles, forgiving sins, and healing people. He has frustrated the hell out of the religious establishment in the process: eating with sinners, tax collectors, and other undesirables, and (more to the point) challenging the authority of the Pharisees—in the Jerusalem temple of all places!

They seek their revenge in the same setting. When Jesus appears at the temple, the Pharisees haul out a woman who was caught having an affair. In front of a big crowd they put Jesus on the spot: "Teacher,... this woman was caught in the very act of adultery. The law of Moses says to stone her. What do you say?" (John 8:4–5). But Jesus doesn't take the bait. Instead, He just stoops down and begins writing in the dust with His finger.

This scene has a cinematic quality, like a cool 1970s spaghetti Western. Jesus is the Clint Eastwood figure: a mysterious itinerant preacher who rolls through town wearing a poncho and a cowboy hat, a little cigarillo dangling from his lip. The lynch mob brings out an accused woman and demands she be punished. Cue the tumbleweeds and Sergio Leone sound track...

So there Jesus is, kneeling down and drawing in the dirt. But the crowd gets really aggressive, demanding an answer. Finally, He stands up and says, "All right, stone her" (John 8:7). Period. Boom. Right there in the temple. Then, after a dramatic pause, He adds: "But let those who have never sinned throw the first stones!" (v. 7). And with that, He stoops down again and continues writing in the dust.

There is a lot of speculation about *what* Jesus was writing in the dust. Maybe it was the sins of the people in the mob: *Such and such a person cheated in business; this guy slept with that other guy's wife*...that sort of thing. We don't know for sure, and it doesn't really matter. What we do know is that Jesus' response completely confounds the woman's accusers. Little by little, they lose their lust for vengeance. John tells us, "They slipped away one by one, beginning with the oldest, until only Jesus was left in the middle of the crowd with the woman" (8:9).

(When I was a kid, at Heritage USA we used to perform this scene on a big public stage. I always played one of the bloodthirsty mob. We grabbed stones and rushed at the woman, yelling, "Stone her! Do it!" Then Jesus would come in and say, "Go ahead, but let the one who never sinned cast the first stone." We would all slowly drop our stones [*plunk, plunk*] and walk away [*plunk*], nice and dramatic. It was powerful, even in this silly theme-park reenactment.)

Once the accusers leave, Jesus stands up again from His dust graffiti and turns to the woman. "Where are your accusers?" He asks. "Don't even one of them condemn you?"

"No, Lord," she answers.

"Neither do I," Jesus says. "Go and sin no more" (see John 8:9–11).

Now this line, "sin no more," has always given me trouble. The whole point of this story is that He is calling everyone out as sinners—not one of us is pure enough to cast the first stone. So I don't think He expects the adulteress to be perfect from then on. But Jesus is looking out for her best interests. He is trying to discourage her from doing things that will harm herself and others.

What's important is that He doesn't join the mob of condemners. Instead, He stands with her, against the crowd. That is restoration. It means siding with the people who have failed and fallen and stumbled. It means loving them, not rejecting them, and then standing by them. That's true strength. And it's exactly what is required to really transform people.

Restoration isn't easy. The fact is that the minute you restore something (whether a classic car or a person), it starts falling apart all over again. It requires constant effort. You don't change people by intimidation (not for the better, anyway). As Martin Luther King Jr. said: "Darkness cannot drive out darkness; only light can do that. Hate cannot drive out hate; only love can do that."

In the end, He's not a Clint Eastwood Jesus at all, but something more like a Gandhi Jesus or a Martin Luther King Jr. Jesus. Love is Christ's only weapon, but He's got limitless ammunition.

With Passion

Restoration can't be done out of obligation or pity. It requires compassion—not just sympathy but empathy, genuine fellow-feeling. The word *compassion* literally means "to suffer with."[2] *Passion* refers to the suffering (physical, spiritual, and mental) that Christ experienced during His crucifixion and death; the prefix *com* means "with" or "together." Through *com-passion* we "suffer with" others; we feel their pain. Together.

Compassion opens up a whole new way of being in the world. We know that we would go to great lengths to avoid our own pain and suffering (as best we can figure out how to, anyway). Through compassion, we do the same thing for others. At a minimum, we avoid compounding suffering by casting stones and piling on when others screw up. Through compassion, we want to alleviate others' suffering as urgently as our own.

It's interesting to note that Paul himself, elsewhere in his writings, struggles to show compassion. In the First Letter to the Corinthians he urges his Christian brothers to excommunicate a church member who is found sleeping with his stepmother: "Why haven't you removed this man from your fellowship?" he asks (5:2). "It certainly is your job to judge those inside the church who are sinning in these ways" (5:12).

Even here there is hope for restoration, but it's pretty harsh: "You must cast this man out of the church and into Satan's hands, so that his sinful nature will be destroyed and he himself will be saved when the Lord returns" (5:5). It is awfully tough tough-love.

This Scripture is so easily abused that, frankly, I wish Paul had never said it. This is the line that is used to kick kids out of the house when they break the rules, and to banish people from churches. It shows that even Paul, the Apostle of Love, let his anger get the better of him from time to time. But you've got to read the story all the way to its conclusion to see how things turn out.

In his Second Letter to the Corinthians, Paul thinks better

of his earlier advice and urges his followers to restore the same man.[3] "He was punished enough when most of you were united in your judgment against him," Paul writes. "Now it is time to forgive him and comfort him. Otherwise he may become so discouraged that he won't be able to recover. Now show him that you still love him" (2 Cor. 2:6–8).

Too often, Christians are all about brotherly love until somebody slips up. Then it's like they're dead to us. There's no place for them in our pews or in our prayers. We abandon them at precisely the time they most need us. Guess what happens? Just as Paul suggests, people do become discouraged. They aren't able to recover.

GRACE NOTE

My friend Brian Yarbrough, who runs Anchor Church in Houston, submitted a story that encapsulates this painful reality and shows us the alternative of unwavering love in one man's life.[4] I want to share it with you:

I never knew someone who was gay until I met Patrick. And I never knew that Patrick was gay until he was banished from our church. For whatever reason, "gay" or "straight" never meant anything to me; probably because we didn't talk about sexuality in an open way in my Texas town, especially in church.

Patrick was our youth leader, though he didn't exactly fit into our middle-class, suburban, churchgoing world. He was six foot six with pale skin and bright red hair styled in one of those New Wave swoops that was shaved underneath.

He was more than just a youth leader to me, he was my friend. We shared stories and struggles for the two years that he was a part of our group. I was twelve years old at the time, and I was struck by how Patrick was willing to listen to my friends and me. He actually seemed to care about what we said and what was going on in our lives when no other adults did.

Suddenly, without explanation, Patrick was forced to leave his role as youth leader. I later learned that someone had found out that he was in a relationship with a man. (I don't know how people find out about these things, it's not as if it was a topic of conversation during our meetings.) Officially, we were told that he was unable to continue because of some "personal problems." The problem, it turns out, was the person he was.

I tried to keep in contact with Patrick over the years. He moved to Portland and, through the internet, we exchanged e-mails every once in a while. Then we lost touch. Through some mutual contacts, I found out that he had died. I couldn't believe that he was gone. I never got the chance to see him again and say good-bye.

Patrick had contracted HIV from the same guy he was dating all those years ago. Rather than leave his boyfriend when he found out that he was sick, Patrick decided to stay to the very end. They had stayed together all that time. Talk about a demonstration of love!

I still can't reconcile the way that my friend was treated by my church, especially when you compare it to the love that he showed in his personal life. I could not understand how God's love for Patrick would be more fickle than Patrick's unwavering commitment to the man he loved.

Patrick was cast off, as though he was "infecting" those around him. I can tell you the only thing that I contracted from the whole experience was a disdain for people whose love is closed off to situations and people they don't understand.

Even in his absence, Patrick serves as a constant reminder to me that we are instructed to draw people into our community at whatever cost. This is how we show the love that God has for us.

—Brian from Texas

Logjam

Paul has little patience for judgment of the sort practiced against Patrick. He writes in Galatians: "If you think you are too important to help someone in need, you are only fooling yourself. You are really a nobody" (6:3). All that other stuff we use to determine our worth in God's eyes doesn't matter if we can't find the compassion to help a brother or sister in a time of need.

If you want to concern yourself with anybody's failures, Jesus instructs us, start with your own. There's plenty to occupy you there. "Why worry about a speck in your friend's eye when you have a log in your own? How can you think of saying, 'Friend, let me help you get rid of that speck in

your eye,' when you can't see past the log in your own eye?"
(Matt. 7:3–4).

The first step is to see our own shortcomings clearly.
Recognizing our own flaws and temptations is the root of
restoration. It's only through an understanding of our own
imperfection—the idea of *There but for the grace of God go
I*—that we find the patience and compassion to restore others instead of condemning and dismissing them.

As Christians, we tend to reserve a special place in
the hell-of-our-hearts for preachers who slip up. After all,
they're the ones who are supposed to provide spiritual guidance and moral direction. They're required to be doubly
perfect. Right?

The fact that they do screw up—often more flagrantly
than their followers—is proof that we're all fallible, we all
fall. Obviously, this is an issue that hits close to home for me.
My parents were the toast of the evangelical church; then
they were just toast.

It goes without saying that their shortcomings made
them bad candidates to be the poster family for Christian
America that they set themselves up to be. But I think about
the difference it would have made in my parents' lives—to
say nothing of mine and my sister's—if more people would
have taken the time to restore them and help them work
through the problems that led them to make some bad
choices.

I saw echoes of my family's experience in the more recent tribulations of Ted Haggard. In 2006, Haggard was
riding high: he was a successful pastor of the mega New
Life Church in Colorado and the outspoken president of

the country's most influential Christian conservative organization, the National Association of Evangelicals. He was practically the big brother of the good sons. His job was to police American politics to ensure that people were abiding by (his conservative interpretation of) God's law.

...That is, until a male prostitute came forward to accuse Haggard of gay sex and drug use, causing Haggard to resign in November 2006.

Now, I don't want to make light of the shock this revelation must have caused Haggard's conservative friends and followers. Of course we're going to be surprised when a preacher who rails against homosexuality turns out to be gay, or when someone who preaches against infidelity is having an affair. Of course we're going to see the hypocrisy in that. But we have to be very careful in how we react to it. God doesn't crumple people up and throw them away because they fail to live up to their public image, and neither should we.

When Haggard's secret came out, he tried counseling. He tried to "recover" in order to resume preaching. (He confessed to Oprah that it didn't work.) He tried to make amends with his family and the church.

What was he told? *Don't come back. Go get a normal job. Go do something else. Become a counselor or something, but DO NOT come back to this congregation. There's no place for you here.*

What he needed was restoration. What he got was a one-way bus ticket across the state line. That's right—he was exiled, run out of town. His church board literally required him to leave the state in exchange for a severance package. (What is this, the Wild West? *This town ain't big enough for both of us*...) Where's the grace in that?

I know what it is to fear the judgment of your congregation. When my wife, Amanda, and I decided to get divorced, I was humiliated and humbled. But I came to Revolution Church and talked to the congregation about it openly. Boy, was I scared. We turned off the recording equipment that we typically use to share the sermons on iTunes so that we could have an intimate discussion.

I told the folks at Revolution about how difficult this time had been for me, how I was really struggling with the reality that my marriage had fallen apart. I honestly didn't know how they'd react. I braced for the worst.

You know what they did? They clapped. It was a little embarrassing, actually. They applauded to support me and to thank me for sharing my struggles with them. They let me know that whatever was going on in my life, I was welcome and appreciated. They gave me the permission to be broken and still be loved.

That simple act of support made a huge difference for me at a difficult time. It confirmed, yet again, the healing potential of grace.

Think about how things might have turned out differently if Ted Haggard's congregation had shown him grace. What if, instead of thinking about how his behavior reflected poorly on them, they had said, "Ted has been a leader and a shepherd to us for years now. We're going to return the favor by standing with him and restoring him"? What a symbol that offering of grace could have been! What a (missed) opportunity to show the bigness of God's love!

I know there are a lot of "ifs, ands, and buts" in a situation like this. There were a lot of hurt feelings. I wasn't part of the congregation, so I don't know how they felt. But that's what dying to yourself is: putting aside your personal hurt and embarrassment and ego to help someone who needs your support.

We tend to hide our brokenness from others precisely because we're afraid of how they will react. In doing so, we give sin its power. But we can take that power away as well. If Haggard hadn't been banished, but instead embraced, his congregation could have given themselves permission to fail and still belong. They could have let grace work in their lives.

The idea that somehow Christians who serve God have it all together just isn't realistic. No more so than expecting flawlessness from the rest of us. Even Saint Francis of Assisi warned against thinking he was perfect. Not long before his death, after a life of saintly acts like rebuilding the church, healing people, and demonstrating an almost supernatural connection with God's wild creatures, he told one of his followers: "Don't be too quick to canonize me. I am perfectly capable of fathering a child."

That goes double for those of us who aren't in line for sainthood. If you find out that I've made a mistake, don't be surprised. I'm one sip away from becoming a raging alcoholic again. I'm one breath away from making any number of mistakes. We all are.

But when we make bad choices, God wants to see us raised back up. He wants to see us restored. Paul's message in Galatians 6 is that we human beings are the instruments of that grace. "Don't get tired of doing what is good," he writes. "Don't get discouraged and give up, for we will reap a harvest of blessing at the appropriate time" (v. 9). We've already quoted 1 Corinthians: "Love never gives up" (13:7). That applies doubly to individuals. Don't give up on them. Don't lose hope in them. Show them grace and restore them.

Chapter 13

Higher Law

How can you sing of amazing grace and all God's wonders without using your hands?

—*Mahalia Jackson*

S hare each other's troubles and problems, and in this way obey the law of Christ," Paul writes in Galatians 6:2. It's an interesting phrase: "the law of Christ." This is the first time Paul has used it. Up to this point, the word *law* has always referred to the law of Moses. Law was something that competed with grace. But here, Jesus takes the law of Moses and brings it into the new covenant with God. He makes it less about rules and more about love. He reinterprets law in light of God's gift of grace.

Turned upside down, the law of Moses becomes the law of Christ. Compare the two side by side: The law of Moses is a rulebook for appeasing God, a guideline for earning our salvation. It is about drawing lines: you're either in or out, saved or damned. Christ's law says that earning salvation is impossible. Because no man is innocent, no man is guilty. We're all pardoned. We're all saved.

The law of Moses demanded obedience and judgment—the faithful were deputized to serve as the long arm of God's law. Contrast that with the lines from Romans: "All have sinned; all fall short of God's glorious standard. Yet now God in his gracious kindness declares us not guilty" (3:23–24). The law of Christ urges universal restoration: We are enlisted to heal.

This contrast sets the stage for the grand finale of Paul's contentious argument with the "legalists" who would require us to follow the letter of the law to achieve salvation.

Surpassing Law

Paul has already shown that if you try to fulfill the law on its own terms, you are bound to fail. Now he crescendos with the idea that grace doesn't just fulfill the law of Moses—it surpasses it.

Starting out in a conciliatory tone, Paul states that there is no conflict with the law here, "for the whole law can be summed up in this one command: 'Love your neighbor as yourself'" (Gal. 5:14).

This sets Paul's endgame in motion. The entirety of the law, he argues, can be boiled down to one simple rule, the "golden rule": love your neighbor as yourself; treat others as you would be treated. It all boils down to love. By equating law with love, Paul reminds us of the words Jesus delivered in the Sermon on the Mount.

Jesus too was speaking to an audience that was anxious

about violating the law of Moses. He first attempted to ease their concerns: "Don't misunderstand why I have come," Jesus says. "I did not come to abolish the law of Moses or the writings of the prophets. No, I came to fulfill them. I assure you, until heaven and earth disappear, even the smallest detail of God's law will remain until its purpose is achieved" (Matt. 5:17–18).

These would seem to be comforting words to the Pharisees in the audience. (*Finally, this rebel is getting with the program!*) But this is really just a setup for Jesus' true message: "But I warn you," He continues, "unless you obey God better than the teachers of religious law and the Pharisees do, you can't enter the Kingdom of Heaven at all!" (5:20). (Take that, Pharisees!)

Jesus goes on to elaborate what this higher standard—made possible by love—looks like. He ticks off the list one by one, updating the rules as He goes:

Of murder and anger, He says: "You have heard that the law of Moses says, 'Do not murder. If you commit murder, you are subject to judgment.' But I say, if you are angry with someone, you are subject to judgment!" (5:21–22).

Of adultery, He says: "You have heard that the law of Moses says, 'Do not commit adultery.' But I say, anyone who even looks at a woman with lust in his eye has already committed adultery with her in his heart" (5:27–28).

Of revenge, He says: "You have heard that the law of Moses says, '[an eye for an eye and a tooth for a tooth].' But I say, don't resist an evil person! If you are slapped on the right cheek, turn the other, too" (5:38–39).

Even before we reconcile ourselves with God, we are

instructed to reconcile with one another: "So if you are standing before the altar in the Temple, offering a sacrifice to God, and you suddenly remember that someone has something against you, leave your sacrifice there beside the altar. Go and be reconciled to that person. Then come and offer your sacrifice to God" (5:23–24).

Of love, He says: "You have heard that the law of Moses says, 'Love your neighbor' and hate your enemy. But I say, love your enemies! Pray for those who persecute you! In that way, you will be acting as true children of your Father in heaven" (5:43–45).

Jesus says that He has come to fulfill the law, and this is how He does it: by replacing law with love. He sets a new standard, one that far exceeds the old standard of obligation. Love exceeds law, and it applies to everyone: "If you love only those who love you, what good is that?" Jesus asks. "Even corrupt tax collectors do that much. If you are kind only to your friends, how are you different from anyone else? Even pagans do that" (5:46–47).

In the end, Jesus calls us to a higher standard: perfection through love. "You are to be perfect, even as your Father in heaven is perfect" (5:48). Motivated by God's grace, you are touched by His perfection. When you act out of love you are, in this small way, perfect. But achieving this standard requires that we reject all the received rules and be guided instead by the inspiration of the Holy Spirit. Paul puts it this way: "Don't copy the behavior and customs of this world, but let God transform you into a new person by changing the way you think. Then you will know what God wants you to do" (Rom. 12:2).

God Is Love

Grace is the evidence of God's love. So too love is evidence that we have received and we comprehend grace. We read in 1 John: "God is love, and all who live in love live in God, and God lives in them. And as we live in God, our love grows more perfect" (4:16–17).

The opposite is equally true. "Anyone who does not love does not know God—for God is love" (4:8). If we aren't showing love, we don't comprehend grace. Our faith isn't bearing fruit in our lives. We somehow didn't get the memo.

Through love, however, we gain a remarkable, almost superhuman power. There's a great line from Saint Augustine that gets at this idea: "For love, everything is easy." Think about the most daunting task you can imagine in life: climbing a mountain, for instance. Most of us dread the idea. But there are people for whom it is a pleasure, who approach the task from a place of joy and exhilaration. Every frostbitten step, every strained breath of altitude-thinned air is energizing because they have the proper inspiration to tackle the challenge. They do it for recreation (*re*-creation). They do it with love.

Grace can give us the inspiration to scale the mountains in our lives. We can take on the hardest tasks with pleasure and confidence knowing that we are undertaking them selflessly and lovingly, with God on our side. With Abba in our *insides*—acting in and through us.

Martin Luther puts the same idea another way: "If we could apprehend [grace] with sure and steadfast faith then no rage or terror of the world, law, sin or death or the devil could be so great that it could not be swallowed up just as a little drop of water is swallowed up to the sea."[1] For love, anything is possible.

The Kingdom

Governed by this new law, the law of love, we arrive at our final destination: the place where our revolutionary road has been leading all along. Paul calls it "the Kingdom of God" (Gal. 5:21).

The phrase may call to mind images of angels strumming harps on cotton-puff clouds. But Paul has something different in mind. He's not talking about an afterlife or a distant future. We aren't asked to sacrifice now so that we can reap a later reward. Paul is concerned with a much more proximate, human, and earthly concept.

In Romans, he writes: "For the Kingdom of God is not a matter of what we eat or drink, but of living a life of goodness and peace and joy in the Holy Spirit. If you serve Christ with this attitude, you will please God. And other people will approve of you, too. So then, let us aim for harmony in the church and try to build each other up" (14:17–19).

The kingdom is to be found in the fruit of the spirit: in a life of goodness, peace, and joy. Harmony in the church and in the broader world. We find the kingdom among people, in the here and now.

If you don't believe Paul, just ask Jesus. We read in the Gospel of Luke: "One day the Pharisees asked Jesus, 'When will the Kingdom of God come?' Jesus replied, 'The Kingdom of God isn't ushered in with visible signs. You won't be

able to say, "Here it is!" or "It's over there!" For the Kingdom of God is among you'" (17:20–21).

That's great news. We don't have to wait for death or the
Second Coming. As my good friend Peter Rollins likes to
say, what's more important than believing in life after death
is believing in life *before* death. We don't have to pine away
our whole lives to be ushered into the kingdom. It's right
in front of our noses. But how do we find it? Where do
we look? "Among you." It's here, now. Among us and between us. The King James Version of the Bible interprets the
phrase as "within you"—it's actually found inside ourselves.
The kingdom exists when we love one another. We bring it
into being when we live in harmony. We enter by the gate-
way of grace.

Through Christ's sacrifice we establish a new relationship
with God. Through this new relationship we are reborn
as risen men. Guided by the Holy Spirit, we bear fruit of
goodness and patience and joy. We rise to fulfill the higher
law of love. Governed by love, we live in harmony with one
another.

That's grace in a nutshell.

Chapter 14

Grace Test and Taillights

I refuse to label people...God don't make no junk.

—*Tammy Faye Bakker*

If you ever wonder whether some attitude or behavior is consistent with grace and its revolutionary implications, try the following thought experiment: Picture the thing that you see Christians doing in the name of Jesus, then substitute Christ (beard, sandals, stigmata, and all) thinking and acting the same way.

If it doesn't seem credible—or worse, if it's downright ridiculous—the action in question is probably on the wrong track.

I try this test when I go to gay pride rallies and see Christians lining the street holding placards that say things like: "GOD HATES YOU," or "HOMOSEXUALITY IS AN ABOMINATION." I try to imagine Jesus standing alongside them wearing a big sandwich board painted with the message "I

HATE YOU." I can't help but laugh (though it would be a lot funnier if it weren't so tragic). Unfortunately, this image of Jesus is precisely what some conservative Christians would have us believe.

Vince, another pastor at Revolution Church, has a T-shirt that does a great job of exposing our misconceptions on this issue. The front of the T-shirt reads "What did Jesus say about homosexuality? Answer on back."

But when you turn around, the back is blank. That's right: Jesus cared so much about homosexuality that He mentioned it exactly zero times. He thought it so central to His message of love, so fundamental to His mission of redeeming the world, that He never touched on the issue in the course of His entire public ministry. Yet, somehow, this single issue has come to define the Christian church in many people's lives.

What I love about the "answer on back" T-shirt is that it forces Christians to confront their misunderstanding of Scripture and grapple with the sources of their ideas. Before seeing the back, people's minds scrawl all sorts of ungracious messages with their mental Sharpie pens: "Sinner. Abomination. Fag. Unnatural."

Then you see the bafflement on their faces when they're confronted with the fact that their Savior saw no reason to even mention homosexuality. Confusion quickly turns to anger. People think they've been tricked—and they're right, but not in the way they think. They've been tricked into compromising grace for a lie.

Gay participation in the church gets to the root of the law vs. grace debate more directly (and certainly more emotionally) than any other issue in our culture today. As we'll see, both sides lay claim to our friend Paul for their respective teams. But in the same way that we challenged ourselves to interpret God through Christ, we've got to see Paul through Christ.

I believe his message of grace is the answer.

For conservative Christians, homosexuality has become a rallying cry and recruitment tool. It's something to get the troops fired up about. For non-Christians, it is an equally blunt instrument: a single-issue indictment of the church, one that makes a mockery of all the Christian talk of love and understanding.

I see it more as a test—a grace test—for us as individuals and for Christianity as a whole. Just as former generations in the church had to overcome their supposedly "God endorsed" racist and sexist attitudes, so we have to overcome our narrow-mindedness on this issue in order to experience (and share) the full potential of grace.

No Junk

Before diving into the specific scriptural references to homosexuality (which we'll do in the next chapter), let me start by saying that I understand how difficult this issue can be for Christians to confront. How are we supposed to make sense of Bible passages that seem to condemn homosexuality and a conclusion (God hates gay people) that is so blatantly at odds with Christ's message of love?

In our confusion, it is all too easy to just follow the crowd and compromise on love and grace. I have struggled with it myself. Like many evangelical Christians in the South, I was taught that homosexuality is about as cut-and-dried as sin gets. Gays were on the fast track to hell.

Fortunately, I had to grapple with the issue early on in life. To be honest, I didn't handle it very well. But thankfully I had someone there to guide me.

When I was thirteen, I had a best friend named Eric (name changed to protect his privacy) in Orlando with whom I used to get into all kinds of trouble. You know, typical bad-kid-in-a-small-town stuff: We'd walk around the cul-de-sac smoking cigarettes; we'd sneak out of the house to smoke a joint or go see the midnight screening of *The Rocky Horror Picture Show.*

Then, one day when we were just standing around smoking, Eric said, "Hey, Jay, there's something I want to tell you . . ." Long pause . . .

"Jay, I think I'm gay," he finally said.

Eric was visibly nervous; I can only imagine how worried he must have been over how I'd react. I'm sad to say that his fears were justified.

Here he was finally revealing the biggest secret in his life to the person he considered to be his best friend. And what did I say? "Sorry, Eric, gotta go."

That was my response in full.

My brain just couldn't process it. (*What? Eric! Gay!?*) It was too much for me to handle, so I ran away. I literally ran. I went straight home and cried my eyes out, not knowing what to do or how to feel about it.

When my mom came home she found me in a puddle of tears.

"Jay, are you okay?" she asked.

"No, Mom," I said through sobs.

"What's wrong?" she asked with growing concern.

"Eric's gay," I answered.

"But is he okay?" she asked, not quite understanding. "Did something happen to him?"

I'm like, Whaddya mean, *Is he okay?*: "He's *gay*, Mom. He likes *guys!*"

"Well, okay," she said, "but what has changed about him?"

She was right, of course. Nothing had changed about him. He was still Eric, the same guy I had spent all that time with. The same guy who had introduced me to the Cure and Depeche Mode albums. The same friend who saw past my family controversy and all my hang-ups when other kids snickered behind my back.

Eventually, I pulled myself together and, with the help of my mom, got over my prejudice. But Eric coming out was a turning point for me—the start of my becoming a "straight ally" (as heterosexual supporters of gay rights are so awkwardly called). It took some time, but I eventually got there.

In high school, I got picked on for hanging out with "the gay guy." "You better watch it," kids would taunt me. "He's going to make a move on you." Fortunately, I was just stubborn and confrontational enough to dig in my heels and fight back. But I'm sure that if it hadn't been for my mom's setting a good example, I would have reacted just like everybody else.

I'm grateful that God has given me the clarity to see gay

rights as a justice issue, a civil rights issue—a grace issue. Just to be clear: I am not saying that homosexuality is a sin that should be accepted because of grace. I don't believe that being gay is a sin. But it is going to take a lot of God's grace for the church to get clear on that and behave accordingly. In championing gay rights within the Christian community, I feel blessed to be building on my mother's legacy.

Mom was from a different generation, so she never came out and said that homosexuality wasn't a sin or anything. But she was a gay ally, no doubt about it. She used to go to gay pride rallies and lead people in singing "Jesus Loves Me, This I Know." She conducted the first interview with someone with AIDS on Christian television back in 1983, as well as the first interview on Christian television with an openly gay minister.

The affection was mutual. Against all odds, my mom—a straight Christian housewife and mother of two—became a gay icon. The gay community adored her. Still does. As I mentioned in chapter 9, RuPaul narrated an entire film about my mom titled *The Eyes of Tammy Faye.*

A gay friend of mine once asked, "Why do you think gay people love your mom so much?"

"Probably because of the makeup and the eyelashes and stuff," I answered, never having given it much thought.

"No," he said. "It's because she's a survivor. No matter what people say about her, no matter what happens to her, she survives."

Zero Tolerance

I'm constantly amazed at how binary the issue is for many Christians. You can do everything else "right"—you can be the most upstanding, devout, and celebrated Christian—but the minute you're gay, you're done. If you're outed, you're out...of the church and God's favor (at least that's what we're led to believe).

That's exactly what happened to my friend the Reverend Mel White. He was practically the dot at the center of the inner circle of the evangelical movement. He was an evangelical minister, a seminary professor, a filmmaker, and a prolific writer of Christian books. During the 1980s, he was the "go-to" ghostwriter for the Christian Right, the man behind books "by" Billy Graham, D. James Kennedy, Ollie North, Pat Robertson, Jerry Falwell, and, yes, Jim and Tammy Faye Bakker.

Mel was also gay (albeit secretly, at the time).

As you might imagine, these two worlds didn't easily coexist. Mel struggled for decades to try to overcome his attraction toward men. He did everything the church prescribed: prayer, psychotherapy—even exorcism and electric shock! He married a woman and had a family (with whom he is still very close) in denial of his sexual orientation. Nothing worked.

When Mel finally decided to embrace being gay in the 1990s, he did a brave thing. He didn't allow his faith to be taken from him. Instead, he and his partner, Gary Nixon, founded Soulforce, an organization that uses the nonviolent principles of Martin Luther King Jr. and Gandhi to fight for equal treatment for sexual minorities within the church.

In his *Letter from Birmingham Jail*, Dr. King wrote that the church too often serves as a "taillight" for society "rather than a headlight leading men to higher levels of justice."[1] King was a headlight for African-American civil rights at a time when the majority of America's faith leaders stood in the way of progress. It is up to people of faith to be the headlights once again, this time for gay civil and religious rights. Mel is one of the brightest lights out there.

Family Outing

I recently joined Mel and Soulforce for a project called "The American Family Outing." Along with a group of gay, lesbian, and transgendered Christian families, I traveled around the country attempting to meet some of America's most popular pastors and biggest congregations. Our mission was simple: have a meal and a conversation—Christians to Christians, parents to parents—to try to dispel some of the fears and misconceptions people have about homosexuality.

One of the places we visited (or tried to, anyway) was California's Saddleback Church, home of Rick Warren.

Warren is arguably America's most influential Christian. His book *A Purpose Driven Life* has sold more copies than any book except the Bible. He was even tapped to give the invocation at President Obama's inauguration. I had high hopes for our visit with Warren. I admire his "purpose-driven" ministry and the work he does to combat AIDS and malaria in Africa. I like his cuddly image and even the goofy oversized Hawaiian shirts he wears. Which is why our visit was so disappointing.

In a video address before Election Day 2008, Warren urged his flock of millions to stop same-sex marriage in California by voting for Proposition 8: "If you believe what the Bible says about marriage, you must support Proposition 8," he declared on his website.[2] In an interview with Beliefnet founder Steve Waldman, he went further, likening gay marriage to polygamy, incest, and pedophilia.[3]

According to Warren, I'm a walking contradiction. I'm an evangelical Christian pastor. I believe in what the Bible says. I believe that Jesus died on the cross. I believe He rose in three days. I believe that in doing so He forgave us our sins. But it is precisely because of these beliefs that I am compelled to stand up for my gay brothers and sisters in Christ. It was in hopes of delivering that message that I went to California with Soulforce.

At first, it looked like the meeting with Warren was going to happen. After a year of negotiations, we were scheduled to attend a service and have dinner with Rick, his wife, Kay, and some Saddleback congregants over Father's Day weekend. It would have been a beautiful symbol of grace in action. But all that changed when *Newsweek* ran a one-line mention that Warren was welcoming "gay dads" to his church. Warren freaked out. He responded in the press that the claim was "100% false": "We did not invite this group and I will not be meeting with them," he wrote on the GetReligion blog.[4]

Ultimately, Warren agreed to meet with one of our families, but it wasn't the open-minded exchange that we had hoped for or expected. The meeting was arranged to take place at a remote satellite campus forty-five minutes from

Saddleback's main church and far from the prying eyes of conservatives or the press. I was not allowed to attend, but it sounds like I didn't miss much. It was about as personal as a book signing. Warren said hello, shook hands, and moved them along. There was no growth in understanding.

The silver lining to our discouraging trip was that it put us in California on June 17, 2008, the day the state began issuing marriage licenses to gay couples. I had the honor of presiding over my first gay wedding, that of my friends Paige and Katie. They had already been in a committed relationship for years; their five-year-old son, Waylon (named after the outlaw country singer), served as ring bearer.

Instead of "man and wife" I pronounced Paige and Katie "married for life." But I may have spoken too soon. With the passage of Proposition 8, the fate of Paige and Katie's marriage—and thousands of others—was thrown to the California courts.

Chapter 15

Exiles in the Kingdom

To banish anger altogether from one's breast is a difficult task. It cannot be achieved through pure personal effort. It can be done only by God's grace.

—Mohandas Gandhi

One of the projects Mel White and Soulforce have taken on is to challenge the shallow interpretation of the Bible that fundamentalist and literalist Christians promote when it comes to homosexuality.

It's an uphill battle for the obvious reason that fundamentalists have already staked out (and popularized) their interpretation. But Mel's got numbers on his side: of the approximately one million verses in the Bible, only six or seven appear to condemn same-sex behavior in any way; meanwhile, there are literally thousands of references to love and compassion. And, as we'll see, even the Scriptures that fundamentalists commonly cite to reject gays and lesbians are more nuanced than is generally understood.

There's more (and less) to the Bible's take on homosexuality than we've been led to believe. The root of the problem is that modern readers often don't take the time to understand what they're reading, let alone to wrap their heads around the context in which the Scriptures were written.

Clobber Scriptures

The simple biblical fact is that Old Testament references in Leviticus (18:22 and 20:13) *do* treat homosexuality as a sin...a capital offense, even. But before you say "I told you so," consider this: Eating shellfish, cutting your sideburns, and getting tattoos were equally prohibited by ancient religious law.

The truth is that the Bible endorses all sorts of attitudes and behaviors that we find unacceptable (and illegal) today and decries others that we recognize as no big deal. Leviticus strictly prohibits interracial marriage; it endorses slavery; and it condones treating women as property. (According to the Old Testament, even women wearing pants is forbidden.) The sexual mores in the Old Testament are especially disturbing to modern readers. Deuteronomy demands that any bride discovered not to be a virgin be stoned to death (22:13–21); that adulterers be summarily executed (22:22); and that when a man dies childless his widow must marry and have sex with the man's brothers until she bears a male heir (25:5–6).

This is not to get down on the Old Testament. It's simply to point out that these laws reflect social concerns of another time and place. Just as our thinking has evolved in these other areas, so it must evolve on the subject of homosexuality. Remember, according to religious law, it's all or nothing: You can't pick and choose the laws that you want to enforce. If you're going to reject homosexuality based on these Scriptures, then you're obligated to keep all these other aspects of the law as well, no matter how outrageous (or illegal according to modern civil law) they might be.

In addition to these Old Testament verses, there are three New Testament verses that are commonly used to convince people that homosexuality is a sin. But under close scrutiny, and placed in their proper context, they too look very different. So much so that in the latest (Third) edition of the Oxford University Press New Revised Standard Version of the Bible, the word *homosexuality* has been removed from the New Testament altogether.[1]

In this translation, the passages (1 Timothy, 1 Corinthians, and Romans) that are commonly thought to refer to homosexuality actually refer to acts like male prostitution, ritual sex, and inhospitality to strangers—all things that Christians discourage, whether gay or straight. There is simply no biblical equivalent to the modern conception of consensual, same-sex, monogamous love between adults.

The first of these "clobber Scriptures" (so called because they're used to beat people over the head) is 1 Timothy 1:10, which says: "These laws are for people who are sexually immoral, for homosexuals [Sodomites] and slave traders, for liars and oath breakers, and for those who do anything else that contradicts the right teaching." The trouble starts when the word *Sodomites* is translated without much thought as "homosexuals." What *Sodomite* actually means is "one who comes from Sodom." So the question becomes: What was the "sin" of Sodom? And what did it have to do with homosexuality?

In Genesis, we are told that the Lord hears of all sorts of wickedness happening in Sodom, so He sends two angels to check it out and help Him decide if the city should be destroyed. Abraham's nephew Lot, who lives in Sodom, greets the angels and invites them into his home. Then, in the middle of the night, "all the men of Sodom, young and old" (Gen. 19:4), surround the house and demand that the angels be brought out so they can be raped.

The really shocking thing—and a detail that seems to be left out when preachers use this story—is that Lot actually offers his *daughters* to the mob instead of the angels: "Look—I have two virgin daughters. Do with them as you wish, but leave these men alone" (Gen. 19:8). Of course, that is not an acceptable solution, but it does say a lot about the motives of the men and boys of Sodom. What we're talking about in this instance is gang rape, not homosexuality. In the ancient world, victorious armies would often rape their defeated enemies to humiliate them. It was an act of power, not just sexuality.

This interpretation is supported by the fact that Jesus and five Old Testament prophets discuss the sins of Sodom without ever once mentioning homosexuality. "Sodom's sins were pride, laziness, and gluttony, while the poor and needy suffered outside her door," writes the prophet Ezekiel (Ezek. 16:49). "She [Sodom] was proud and did loathsome things, so [God] wiped her out, as you have seen" (16:50). In Matthew, Jesus characterizes Sodom's sin as one of inhospitality, but He has nary a word to say about homosexuality (see Matt. 10:11–15). It is for these reasons, not homosexuality, that the city of Sodom was said to be destroyed.

The second of the clobber Scriptures hits a little closer to home for Paul fans. It comes from Paul's First Letter to the Corinthians. In it, Paul warns against sexual immorality, saying, "Don't fool yourselves. Those who indulge in sexual sin, who are idol worshipers, adulterers, male prostitutes, homosexuals, thieves, greedy people, drunkards, abusers, and swindlers—none of these will have a share in the Kingdom of God" (6:9–10).

Here again, though, the text requires a closer look. As Mel White explains, Paul uses the Greek words *malakois* and *arsenokoitai* in 1 Corinthians, which are often mistranslated as "male prostitutes" and "homosexuals" respectively. But the latter, mistaken translation hasn't been around very long. The first time that the word *homosexual* ever appeared in an English-language Bible was in 1958. Greek language scholars have begun to recover the true meaning of the word. *Malaokois*, we now know, probably meant "effeminate call boys"—young hairless men who were used for sexual pleasure. *Arsenokoitai*, meanwhile, referred to the married men who hired them for entertainment. So Paul was talking about prostitutes and the men who hired them, not adults engaged in consensual same-gender love.[2]

Last, let's look at Romans, which is probably the toughest clobber Scripture to address. Paul writes:

[Romans] exchanged the truth of God for a lie, and worshiped and served created things rather than the Creator—who is forever praised. Amen. Because of this, God gave them over to shameful lusts. Even their women exchanged natural relations for unnatural ones. In the same way the men also abandoned natural relations with women and were inflamed with lust for one another. Men committed indecent acts with other men, and received in themselves the due penalty for their perversion. (1:25–27 NIV)

This seems pretty clear, and plenty damning. But there is more to the story. "Paul's Christian contemporaries criticize a range of behaviors common in the pagan world," write the editors of the New Oxford Annotated Bible, in reference to this passage. "Although widely read today as a reference to homosexuality, the language of unnatural intercourse was more often used in Paul's day to denote not the orientation of sexual desire, but its immoderate indulgence, which was believed to weaken the body (*the due penalty*)."[3]

To understand this, we've got to know a little bit about what was going on in Rome at the time. Remember, Christians were a tiny minority among Romans in Paul's day. Most citizens were pagans who worshipped a variety of gods, each with its own ritual practices. Idol worship was commonplace; Roman temples were filled with all kinds of statues of birds and other creatures. Some gods, like Dana, were fertility gods, whose followers worshipped by performing a variety of sexual acts. Priestesses had penis-shaped objects made out of rock, wood, or gold that they used for ritual self-penetration. They had sex with men and women—basically, whoever strolled up to the temple.

This "anything goes" attitude toward sex permeated

many aspects of Roman culture. Caesars, who were literally believed to be gods living among men, would host huge orgies that included rampant hetero- and homo-sex. Prostitution and sex with children was also commonplace. So in condemning these specific sex acts, Paul was challenging an entire pagan worship system that endorsed multiple gods, promiscuity, idol worship, and pedophilia.

Mel White writes: "Responsible homosexuals would join Paul in condemning anyone who uses children for sex, just as we would join anyone else in condemning the threatened gang rape in Sodom or the behavior of the sex-crazed priests and priestesses in Rome."[4] (I've included a list of readings at the end of this book that get into this issue in more depth—on both sides—if you are interested in pursuing these questions further.)

Dueling Scriptures

None of these passages reflect or refer to the modern social or scientific understanding of homosexuality. (As of this writing, I'm working with like-minded groups to start a petition to get Bible publishers to remove the word "homosexuality" from the Bible altogether.) And, even if you still have reservations about particular scripture verses, it's important not to miss the forest for the trees. As Shakespeare wrote, "The devil can cite Scripture for his purpose." When we get lost in the maze of dueling citations and narrow reading of Scripture, we lose sight of the larger point of grace.

We don't want to be like the Pharisees, who failed to

recognize Christ because they were so deep into Scripture, so preoccupied with law, that it became a distraction. In Matthew we read,

> One of [the Pharisees], an expert in religious law, tried to trap [Jesus] with this question: "Teacher, which is the most important commandment in the law of Moses?" Jesus replied, "'You must love the Lord your God with all your heart, all your soul, and all your mind.' This is the first and greatest commandment. A second is equally important: 'Love your neighbor as yourself.' All the other commandments and all the demands of the prophets are based on these two commandments." (22:35–40)

When we strip away religious law, what's left is love—for God and neighbor. This is the core message of Paul's teaching: that Christ's sacrifice on the cross freed us from having to earn God's love and secure our own salvation by following the rules. Once we internalize that idea and understand that is what God wants for our lives, our eyes are opened to see that everyone is invited to salvation through Christ.

Jesus never once mentioned homosexuality, but He had plenty to say about love, respect, compassion, and tolerance for our fellow human. He had little patience for the religious leaders of His day who used Scripture like a bludgeoning tool. But He was tireless in reaching out to groups that religious leaders excluded and damned, including sinners, tax collectors, prostitutes, and nonbelievers. "Stop judging others, and you will not be judged," Jesus says in Matthew (7:1).

He tells us of God's universal acceptance in every way He can think of.

Paul teaches us the same thing. Despite the clobber Scriptures credited to him, Paul's core message is overwhelmingly weighted on the side of grace. In Romans, right after elaborating a list of human failures ("wickedness, sin, greed, hate, envy, murder, fighting, deception,..." [1:29]), Paul warns those who would judge others: "You may be saying, 'What terrible people you have been talking about!' But you are just as bad, and you have no excuse! When you say they are wicked and should be punished, you are condemning yourself, for you do these very same things" (2:1).

As we have seen, the point of Paul's ministry is that the religious law has been replaced by the law of Christ, the law of love: universal acceptance through grace. "You have died with Christ, and he has set you free from the evil powers of this world," Paul writes in Colossians. "So why do you keep on following rules of the world, such as, 'Don't handle, don't eat, don't touch'" (2:20–21). No, he continues, "you must make allowance for each other's faults and forgive the person who offends you. Remember, the Lord forgave you, so you must forgive others" (3:13).

The point is that we must weigh all the evidence. Obviously, Paul had things to say that a lot of people find harsh today. At times, his anger and judgment got the better of him. But his message of grace forces us to a different conclusion: The clobber Scriptures don't hold a candle to the raging inferno of grace and love that burns through Paul's writing and Christ's teaching. And it's this love that should be our guiding light.

When we make people feel unwelcome in our faith communities because of who they are and how they love, we miss the true meaning of Christianity. We place false limits on God's bigheartedness when we organize rallies against gay civil and religious rights. We violate God's principle of unconditional acceptance when we persist in the ill-founded idea that gays should or could deny their orientation in order to belong in our churches.

When we deny grace for others in these ways, we deny Christ and His sacrifice. And when we take the Christ out of Christianity, we're left with a religion that isn't worthy of the name.

The Flames

Imagine for a minute being told by your spiritual advisers and mentors that God hates you. Imagine being told that God condemns the most important and tender human relationships you've found on earth. What would that do to you?

We don't have to imagine because the evidence is well documented. This experience drives gay Christians to the brink of despair . . . and beyond. A recent study published in the journal of the American Academy of Pediatrics found that the rejection of homosexual children by their parents was strongly associated with poor health behaviors. Lesbian, gay, and bisexual kids who grew up with families that did not accept them as gay were far more likely to be depressed, to use illicit drugs, and to have unprotected sex.[5] They were nearly nine times more likely to be suicidal. A spate of recent suicides has brought this tragic pattern into the headlines: in

September 2010 alone, there were four high-profile suicides among gay teenagers due to bullying.

Too often, the excuse for this rejection is Christianity. Many gay Christians lose their faith as a consequence of this rejection. Too many lose their lives. The church almost cost my friend Jef Evans both.

Jef was a counselor in the youth department at First Baptist Church Orlando when I was living in that city during the early 1990s. Each summer the church held a six-week-long summer camp, which my mom saw as a great opportunity to get me out of the house. There were two counselors at the camp: Jef, a closeted, gay, über-Christian; and this other good-looking jock guy. The jock counselor got all the popular kids in his group: the cheerleaders, the athletes, the presidents of church youth groups. Jef got the freaks, geeks, and weirdos. Me included.

I was going through a really rough patch the summer I met Jef. My dad was in prison and I was a full-blown alcoholic floundering in school. Jef was one of the few people associated with the church who made me feel welcome. He didn't treat me as the son of a celebrity (or the son of a pariah); I was just another misfit kid trying to understand my relationship with God and how I fit into the world.

Jef came from an interesting family himself. His grandfather was a well-known preacher for a conservative evangelical denomination called the World Baptist Fellowship. These guys make the Southern Baptists look like lefty liberals: "Don't dance, don't drink, don't smoke, don't chew—don't be seen with those who do," is how he describes the mantra he grew up with.

Growing up in this repressive environment, Jef found he could get all kinds of attention by being a super-righteous Christian kid. He recalls competing in "preacher boy" contests where sermonizing was turned into a sport. (He did well enough to win a little trophy with a book on top that was supposed to be the Bible.) But his concept of God was based mostly in fear. Jef was taught that if he listened to popular music or watched a PG movie, God would punish someone from his family. Not him directly, mind you, but his mom or dad or siblings... that's how cruel and vindictive God was.

Jef swallowed the church's opinions regarding homosexuality hook, line, and sinker—even if those opinions stuck in his gills. "God hates fags," was the lesson as he learned it. Yet Jef couldn't deny his own growing attraction to men. "I was doing everything right," he recalled in a recent talk he gave at Revolution Church in Brooklyn. "I would say to God, 'I don't want this; take this away.'"

After high school, Jef was struggling to straddle the two worlds of his faith and his sexuality. He had had a boyfriend (someone he met in church), and he'd begun to wonder how God could disapprove of a relationship that felt so good and supportive.

It made him question his beliefs. *If God has a problem with this, maybe there's something wrong with my religion*, he thought. But he wasn't ready to give up yet. When he heard that Liberty University (an extremely conservative Christian college founded by Jerry Falwell) had a counseling program for gay students, he decided to go there. *They can help me be straight*, he convinced himself.

Unfortunately, by the time he arrived on campus, Liberty had shut down the counseling program that had drawn him there.

"Liberty is the most ill-named school," Jef said, looking back. "There was nothing liberating about it." He couldn't miss the comedy in the school's athletic team name: the Flames. "I couldn't help but wonder if all the money for the counseling program for Liberty's flaming students was put into the Liberty Flames football team instead."

At the time, however, it was no laughing matter. Jef found himself at Liberty University with nowhere to turn. When he hesitantly confided in a friend that he was gay, she gave him a booklet from Exodus International, an "ex-gay ministry" that tries to cure gay Christians by encouraging them to suppress their sexuality. The booklet taught him to respond to lustful thoughts about men by quoting a Bible verse, singing a hymn, or praying. Suffice it to say, it didn't work. Jef began to see the whole Christian response to homosexuality as "calculated denial." "You're taught to brainwash yourself," he said. In a state of despair, Jef soon failed his classes and dropped out of school. He was so anguished by the judgment he felt from his faith that he contemplated suicide.

One night, he decided to put his fate in God's hands. "God, You've got one more chance or I'm gonna kill myself," he prayed. "I'm gonna flip through the Bible and put my finger on a Bible verse at random. If it speaks to me, I won't kill myself. If not, I will." He landed on a verse in Paul's Second letter to Timothy: "Do not be ashamed to testify about our Lord...Join with me in suffering for the gospel, by the power of God, who has saved us and called us to a holy life" (1:8–9 NIV). He interpreted it as an affirmation of his faith, so he decided to carry on.

Unable to reconcile his sexuality and his religion, Jef began to chip away at his concept of God. He found that the less he believed, the more room he made for himself and the more comfortable he felt. He came out as a gay man and an agnostic at the same time.

I lost track of Jef after he was my counselor. We didn't see each other again for almost fifteen years, until a mutual friend brought me around to a bar where he was sitting having a drink. At first, Jef was reluctant to reintroduce himself for fear that I'd see him as (his words) "a beer-swollen homo atheist in a fag bar." But we picked up right where we'd left off.

Today, Jef jokes that when he first heard that Revolution Church was "gay affirming," he thought it sounded like "an abdominal workout for guys in Chelsea, NYC." But he gave us a shot anyway. He occasionally comes to services, and being surrounded by nonjudgmental Christians has allowed him to begin to explore his faith again. Seeing grace in action has given him hope that there might be a place for him in God's kingdom, and maybe even a place for God again somewhere in his life.

I think that's wonderful. But wherever he ends up, the fact is that God loves him just the same. That's what makes grace so revolutionary.

Chapter 16

Grace Land

If the only prayer you ever say in your entire life is "thank you,"
it will be enough.

—*Meister Eckhart*

Paul vacillates between two emotional extremes in his
letters: Much of the time he is overwhelmed by the
love and peace that come from knowing Christ and receiving grace; at other times, he is desperate and exasperated
that we might reject Christ's sacrifice and turn our backs on
grace.

We see Paul's passion again in the final lines of his Letter to
the Galatians: "Notice what large letters I use as I write these
closing words in my own handwriting" (6:11). It is an intimate moment, one that draws you right into the room with
him. You imagine that Paul has been sitting back dictating this
letter all along to a scribe or a friend. But then he can't stand
it anymore, so he leaps up out of his chair and yanks the quill
(or whatever) away from his assistant and begins scrawling the

conclusion in his own huge graffiti letters at the bottom of the page.

Writing in his own hand, he reiterates his major themes, starting with circumcision: the issue that prompted him to write the letter in the first place. "Those who are trying to force you to be circumcised are doing it for just one reason. They don't want to be persecuted for teaching that the cross of Christ alone can save" (6:12).

Next, Paul reminds us that the law is an impossible standard, and that we cannot hope to achieve salvation that way: "Even those who advocate circumcision don't really keep the whole law" (6:13).

He urges us to forget our pride and to stop trying to impress people: "God forbid that I should boast about anything except the cross of our Lord Jesus Christ. Because of that cross, my interest in this world died long ago, and the world's interest in me is also long dead" (6:14).

What matters is that we are spiritually transformed: "It doesn't make any difference now whether we have been circumcised or not. What counts is whether we really have been changed into new and different people" (6:15).

Finally, Paul reminds us of the peace and harmony that are possible through Grace: "May God's mercy and peace be upon all those who live by this principle. They are the new people of God" (6:16).

New people—that's what Paul challenges us to become. Through grace, it's possible.

Scars of Jesus

These weren't just idle ideas for Paul. He lived them as best he could. He fought for them with all his wit, energy, and strength. Ultimately, he died for them.

We see his tragic end foreshadowed in the second-to-last verse in Galatians. "From now on, don't let anyone trouble me with these things," he writes. "For I bear on my body the scars that show I belong to Jesus" (6:17). Paul's "scars" were all too real. Just as he had persecuted Christians early in his life, Paul was persecuted for espousing grace. Every punishment that he inflicted on others was repaid to him.

In 2 Corinthians, Paul gives us an account of the hardships he endured for grace:

> Five different times the Jews gave me thirty-nine lashes. Three times I was beaten with rods. Once I was stoned. Three times I was shipwrecked. Once I spent a whole night and a day adrift at sea. I have traveled many weary miles. I have faced danger from flooded rivers and from robbers. I have faced danger from my own people, the Jews, as well as from the Gentiles. I have faced danger in the cities, in the deserts, and on the stormy seas. And I have faced danger from men who claim to be Christians but are not. I have lived with weariness and pain and sleepless nights. Often I have been hungry and thirsty and have gone without food. Often I have shivered with cold, without enough clothing to keep me warm. Then, besides all this, I have the daily burden of how the churches are getting along. (11:24–28)

Paul was anxious for the churches because he feared all his work might be in vain. He feared that people would slip back into law and turn their backs on grace. Unfortunately, in many ways, we have.

Martyrdom

In later Christian iconography, Saint Paul is often depicted holding a scroll (symbolizing the Scriptures) and a sword. While the weapon may seem like a fitting emblem for the fearless and combative apostle we've come to know in this book, it actually symbolizes his death at the hands of Rome.

Christian tradition tells us that Paul was beheaded sometime between AD 64 and AD 67, though we don't know much about the events surrounding his death. It appears that he was rounded up in a wave of Christian arrests following the burning of Rome during the reign of Nero. It was illegal to be Christian, so no further charges were required.

Other disciples died in worse ways. James was thrown from the top of the temple and then had his skull crushed with a club; Peter was crucified upside down. (Legend has it that Peter and Paul were killed on the same day.) Paul's comparatively merciful beheading was perhaps because, unlike his fellow apostles, he was a Roman citizen.

We get a sense for Paul's state of mind at the end of his life in his final epistle, 2 Timothy,[1] which was written from prison a few years before. "My life has already been poured out as an offering to God," Paul writes. "The time of my death is near. I have fought a good fight, I have finished the race, and I have remained faithful. And now the prize awaits me" (4:6–8).

Reading these lines, I can't help but think of the haunting words from Martin Luther King Jr.'s final speech, delivered the day before he was killed in Memphis. He talked about cultivating a "dangerous unselfishness": "I don't know what will happen now. We've got some difficult days ahead. But it doesn't matter with me now. Because I've been to the mountaintop...I've seen the promised land. I may not get there with you. But I want you to know tonight, that we, as a people will get to the promised land."[2]

Grace was Paul's promised land—and in a sense he had already arrived. Remember, Paul believed that it was possible to enact the kingdom of heaven even while still here on earth. It is a spiritual place that exists alongside our physical world. Paul's revolution was to show us how—via grace—to get there together.

He ends this, his final letter, with a blessing: "Grace be with you all" (2 Tim. 4:22). It's easy to read this as a throwaway line, but it isn't. He showed us a new vision of God, a new understanding of ourselves, and how to better relate to one another. Paul's revolution was to knock down the gates of the kingdom and usher *everyone* inside.

We've talked a lot about the lack of grace the church has shown to homosexuals because it's such a timely (and egregious) example. But there are all kinds of issues, big and small, that cry out for grace in the world today. We do well to remember grace when we're down and out, or feeling that we've failed. If you've lost your job, or had an affair, or if you're fighting some kind of addiction, grace is there to hold you up. It's there to help you pick up the pieces and build you *back* up.

Grace isn't some lousy crutch. It's more like a bionic limb: Through grace we can be better and stronger than before (*we have the technology*).

You know the phrase "gracious in defeat." But what about *gracious in victory*? If we internalize grace, it can help us temper our excesses of egomania and vanity when things are going our way. God doesn't love us any more in the good times, or love others any less. He demonstrated His love by serving others, especially the downtrodden. He made the ultimate sacrifice: dying for all humankind, whether or not we deserved it. It's when things are going well for us that we need to heed His example and "die to ourselves" a little. Grace can help us keep a level head and cultivate a spirit of generosity toward others when we're riding high on the hog.

The Wages of Grace

It's never too early for grace. Or too late. This is the lesson of the parable of the workers in the vineyard, which Jesus tells in the Gospel of Matthew. It's a great way to conclude our discussion of grace.

"The Kingdom of Heaven is like the owner of an estate who went out early one morning to hire workers for his vineyard," Jesus says (Matt. 20:1). But he didn't hire them all at once. No, the owner hired some workers at the start of the day, and then others at intervals as the day went along: at 9 a.m., noon, 3 p.m., and 5 p.m.

Now, obviously, they all didn't put in the same hours or contribute the same amount of effort. Some had just arrived on the job and rolled up their sleeves to work when the whistle blew and the day was over. But when it came time to pay the workers, the owner did a funny thing: He paid them all a full day's wages regardless of how long or how hard they'd worked.

This didn't sit well with the people who had been busting their butts all day long:

> When they received their pay, [some of the workers] protested, "Those people worked only one hour, and yet you've paid them just as much as you paid us who worked all day in the scorching heat." [The owner answered:] "Friend, I haven't been unfair! Didn't you agree to work all day for the usual wage? Take it and go. I wanted to pay this last worker the same as you. Is it against the law for me to do what I want with my money? Should you be angry because I am kind?" (Matthew 20:11–15)

This is one of the questions grace forces us to confront: Should we be angry because God is kind? Obviously not. We should realize that He doesn't care how much or how little we've done for Him. Grace is a gift we can never pay back or earn or justify—no matter how hard we work.

We can't allow the Christians who have been working at their relationship with God longer than others to get all puffed up with self-righteousness and chase off the newcomers. If you're a longtimer and you've been sweating it out in the fields of faith for years, you should still be grateful for the grace you've received. With the proper mind-set, you should even be glad to see people getting it more easily than you did. Grace is a steal at any price. We should just be grateful to receive it whenever and however and wherever we find it.

The theologian Paul Tillich compares grace to "a wave of light that breaks into our darkness." He writes that "it is as though a voice were saying: 'You are accepted. *You are accepted*, accepted by that which is greater than you." He goes on to write, "After such an experience we may not be better than before, and we may not believe more than before. But everything is transformed... And nothing is demanded of this experience, no religious or moral or intellectual presupposition, nothing but acceptance."[3]

Grace is all about acceptance. By accepting grace we accept God, we accept ourselves, we accept each other.

Grace be with you *all*.

Coauthor Note
by Martin Edlund

I met Jay the way many of us first encountered the Bakkers: through the media. I was working as a freelance writer when an editor-friend at a snarky New York magazine approached me saying, "Have I got a story for you..."

It was easy to see why Jay piqued the editor's interest. The Sundance Channel had just announced a documentary series about the son of the fallen televangelists called *One Punk Under God*. Jay had recently relocated from the South to New York City, where he was preaching Sunday afternoons out of a bar called Pete's Candy Store in the trendy Brooklyn neighborhood of Williamsburg. What's more, Jay was wading into the overheated waters of Christianity's treatment of the gay community.

The story had a lot going for it: drugs, sex, scandal, redemption, 1980s nostalgia. But was it anything more than a curiosity? I was intrigued enough to find out.

As it happened, Jay's famous father, Jim Bakker, was in town the first Sunday I went to Revolution Church. Tammy Faye was in hospice with stage-four cancer, and her illness had motivated the estranged father and son to try to patch things up after two years of not speaking to each other.

I was first struck by the physical resemblance: Jay shares his father's high forehead, slight stature, and quickly drawn mouth. But the differences were equally striking. Jay's pulpit was a rickety music stand set up under bar lights. His vestments were a leather biker jacket, thick Buddy Holly–looking Ray-Ban glasses, and jeans worn rockabilly style with an oversized cuff. The tattoos that start at his collar culminate on his hands with the words *HELP ME LORD* inked one letter per knuckle. He ends his sermons not with his father's famous catchphrase, "God loves you; He really does," but with a reminder to "tip the bartender on your way out..."

Jay didn't speak that day, but instead turned the spotlight over to his dad and sat at the foot of the dinky stage nervously watching his father address the crowd of dread-locked and pierced twenty- and thirty-somethings. "I've never preached in a bar before, so this is liberating," said Jim Bakker, trying to break the ice. He flashed his made-for-TV smile for an instant, before catching himself and swallowing it. "I'm really more nervous *here* than being on television," he confessed. It was easy to believe him.

After the service, I went out to the bar to talk with Jay. I was still skeptical.

Jay was funny, self-deprecating, open, and profound. He obviously brought a lot of baggage with him (he was the first to admit it), but he didn't seem motivated by the need for vindication or anger at what had happened to his family. As he downed a steady stream of Diet Cokes across the table from me (he hasn't had an alcoholic beverage in fifteen years), I began to see qualities I didn't expect, namely courage and humility.

As I got to know Jay better, I would learn that he knows all too well how he appears to the world. He sees the absurdity of being a Bakker and a preacher. He realizes that he isn't photographed for Kenneth Cole ads because of his good looks. When he finds himself on panels at thought-leader events alongside brainiacs like *God Delusion* author Richard Dawkins, he wonders (along with the crowd) what in the world he's doing up there. Jay quotes Paul's First Letter to the Corinthians by way of explaining the position he's found himself in: "God hath chosen the *foolish* things of the world to *confound the wise*" (1:27 KJV, emphasis added).

But it's Jay's confessional style and his very public struggles that make him the one people line up to talk to after these kinds of panels and public events. He is accessible—human in his flaws—in a way that a lot of other preachers and religious thinkers aren't.

His lessons of God and grace didn't come from seminary, but from the theological "School of Hard Knocks." His ministry is transparently a response to his family's mistakes and his on again/off again relationship with the church. This narrative is part of what makes him so compelling: The forces that once drove him away from God are the same ones that compel him to preach today.

Jay isn't trying to emulate his father. If anything, these days, it's the other way around. As that first Sunday sermon at the bar drew to a close—long after the space was supposed to have been turned over to an open-mic singing event—Jim Bakker offered a few parting words about his son.

"I'm so proud of my son. He's doing what I wish I could do. He's loving everybody," Jim said, peering down at Jay through wet eyes. "I want to be more like Jesus, but I really want to be more like Jamie first."

Recommended Reading List

For further insight on grace and the issues addressed in this book, try reading these books that have influenced, challenged, and inspired me:

Armstrong, Karen. *The Bible: A Biography.* New York: Grove Press, 2008.

Brown, Steve. *When Being Good Isn't Good Enough.* Grand Rapids: Baker, 1995.

Caputo, John. *On Religion (Thinking in Action).* New York: Routledge, 2001.

Dark, David. *The Sacredness of Questioning Everything.* Grand Rapids: Zondervan, 2009.

Gregory, A. J. *Messy Faith: Daring to Live by Grace.* Grand Rapids: Revell, 2008.

Jones, Tony. *The New Christians: Dispatches from the Emergent Frontier.* San Francisco: Jossey-Bass, 2009.

Love, Cindi. *Would Jesus Discriminate? The 21st Century Question.* Trafford Publishing, 2008.

Luther, Martin. *Galatians: The Crossway Classic Commentaries.* Wheaton: Good News Publishers, 1998.

Manning, Brennan. *Abba's Child: The Cry of the Heart for Intimate Belonging.* Colorado Springs: NavPress, 2002.

———. *The Ragamuffin Gospel.* Sisters, OR: Multnomah, 1990.

McLaren, Brian D. *A New Kind of Christian: A Tale of Two Friends on a Spiritual Journey.* San Francisco: Jossey-Bass, 2001.

———. *A New Kind of Christianity: Ten Questions That Are Transforming the Faith.* New York: HarperOne, 2010.

———. *The Last Word and the Word After That: A Tale of Faith, Doubt, and a New Kind of Christianity.* San Francisco: Jossey-Bass, 2008.

———. *The Story We Find Ourselves In: Further Adventures of a New Kind of Christian.* San Francisco: Jossey-Bass, 2008.

Nouwen, Henri J. M. *The Return of the Prodigal Son: A Story of Homecoming.* New York: Image, 1994.

———. *The Wounded Healer: Ministry in Contemporary Society.* New York: Image, 1979.

Rollins, Peter. *The Fidelity of Betrayal: Towards a Church Beyond Belief.* Brewster, MA: Paraclete Press, 2008.

———. *How (Not) to Speak of God.* Brewster, MA: Paraclete Press, 2006.

———. *The Orthodox Heretic: And Other Impossible Tales.* Brewster, MA: Paraclete Press, 2009.

Tillich, Paul. *The Courage to Be.* New Haven: Yale University Press, 1952.

———. *The Shaking of the Foundations.* New York: Charles Scribner's Sons, 1948.

Turner, Steve. *The Man Called Cash: The Life, Love and Faith of an American Legend*. London: Bloomsbury, 2005.

White, Mel. *Stranger at the Gate: To Be Gay and Christian in America*. New York: Plume, 1995.

Wills, Gary. *What Paul Meant*. New York: Viking, 2006.

Wilson, A. N. *Paul: The Mind of the Apostle*. New York: W. W. Norton, 1998.

Wright, Robert. *The Evolution of God*. New York: Little, Brown, 2009.

Yaconelli, Michael. *Messy Spirituality*. Grand Rapids: Zondervan, 2007.

Yancey, Philip. *What's So Amazing About Grace?* Grand Rapids: Zondervan, 2002.

Acknowledgments

Jay Bakker would like to thank Tammy Sue Bakker, James and Jonathan Chapman, my co-pastor Reverend Vince Anderson (for being willing to go to hell and back with me), Bo and Shannon Julian, Brennan Manning, Mike Yaconelli, Brian McLaren, Bart Campolo, Tony Jones, Peter Rollins, Steve Brown, Jenn DuHamel (for letting Martin work on the book), David Brokaw, Tony and Peggy Campolo, Mel White, Jeff Lutes, everyone at Soulforce, D. E. Paulk, Stu Damron, Dana Martin, Pete's Candy Store, Randy and Gary Eddy-McCain, Open Door Community Church, Dr. Jack Drescher, and all Revolution Church staff and congregation (past, present, and online).

Martin Edlund would like to thank Jenn DuHamel, Brian Groh, Father Tim Clark, and Donna Edlund for their thoughtful reading and graceful edits of the book.

Notes

Introduction

1. American Religious Identification Survey 2008, http://www.americanreligionsurvey-aris.org/reports/highlights.html.

Chapter 1: Free-Fallin'

1. "Religion, Power, Glory—and Politics," *Time*, February 17, 1986.
2. *The Larry King Show,* March 25, 1987, telecast.

Chapter 2: The Rising

1. "The Last Outlaw Poet," *Rolling Stone*, April 16, 2009.

Chapter 3: Revolutionary Road

1. I would encourage you to go even further and understand a little bit about where the Bible comes from: the time and culture in which it was written. Karen Armstrong's *The Bible* (New York: Grove Press, 2008) is a good introduction.

2. Gary Wills, *What Paul Meant* (New York: Viking, 2006), 138.

3. Romans, Galatians, 1 Corinthians, 2 Corinthians, 1 Thessalonians, Philemon, and Philippians.

4. A. N. Wilson, *Paul: The Mind of the Apostle* (New York: W. W. Norton, 1998), 258.

Chapter 4: Bad Apples

1. Bainton, Roland H., *Here I Stand: A Life of Martin Luther* (Peabody, MA: Hendrickson, 2009), 34.

2. Ibid., 44..

3. Martin Luther, *Galatians: The Crossway Classic Commentaries*, eds. Alistair McGrath and J. I. Packer, (Wheaton, IL: Crossway Books, 1998), 200.

4. Ibid., 200.

5. Bainton, *Here I Stand*, 41.

6. Luther, *Galatians*, 168.

Chapter 5: I Fought the Law

1. Gary Wills, *What Paul Meant* (New York: Viking, 2006).

2. BBC, http://news.bbc.co.uk/2/hi/276677.stm.

3. Mark Driscoll sermon, "Luke: Jesus and Demons," February 14, 2010.

4. *The 700 Club*, September 13, 2001, telecast.

5. Ibid., August 6, 1998, telecast.

6. Ibid., January 13, 2010, telecast.

7. Desiring God blog post, August 20, 2009, http://www.desiringgod.org/Blog/1965_the_tornado_the_lutherans_and_homosexuality/

Chapter 6: Abba

1. Brian D. McLaren, *A New Kind of Christianity: Ten Questions That Are Transforming the Faith* (New York: HarperOne, 2010), 115.
2. Brennan Manning, *Abba's Child: The Cry of the Heart for Intimate Belonging* (Colorado Springs: NavPress, 2002), 62.

Chapter 8: Freaks and Greeks

1. Karen Armstrong, *The Bible: A Biography* (New York: Grove Press, 2008), 27.
2. *South Park* episode 58, "Probably," original air date July 26, 2000.

Chapter 10: Risen Man

1. Luther, *Galatians*,152.
2. Ibid., 151.
3. Ibid., 152.
4. Definition from allwords.com.

Chapter 11: The Fruit

1. I find this is one of the most abused Scriptures, commonly used by Christians to condemn other people to hell. But remember, that's not at all what it's about. Paul is describing this within the context of our freedom to screw up without jeopardizing our salvation.

Chapter 12: Clint Eastwood Jesus

1. Dictionary.com, based on the Random House Dictionary, © Random House, Inc. 2010.

2. Dictionary.com, based on the Random House Dictionary, © Random House, Inc. 2010.

3. There is an ongoing debate among religious scholars about whether it is the same guy or not. I believe it is, but I just wanted you to be aware of the debate.

4. Brian Yarbrough is one of the kindest people I know, and his Anchor Church is a real inspiration. Find out more about it at www.anchorchurchhouston.com.

Chapter 13: Higher Law

1. Luther, *Galatians*, 242.

Chapter 14: Grace Test and Taillights

1. Martin Luther King Jr., *I Have a Dream: Writings and Speeches That Changed the World* (New York: HarperOne, 1992), 96.

2. Beliefnet.com, http://blog.beliefnet.com/progressive revival/2008/10/rick-warren-proposition-8.html.

3. See http://www.beliefnet.com/News/2008/12/ Rick-Warren-Transcript.aspx?p=7#gaymarriage.

4. Get Religion blog, http://www.getreligion.org/?p=3597.

Chapter 15: Exiles in the Kingdom

1. *The New Oxford Annotated Bible: New Revised Standard Version*, 3rd ed.

2. Mel White, *What the Bible Says—and Doesn't Say—About Homosexuality*, http://www.soulforce.org/pdf/whatthe biblesays.pdf.

3. *New Oxford Annotated Bible*, page 245.

4. White, *What the Bible Says*.

5. Caitlin Ryan et al., "Family Rejection as a Predictor of Negative Health Outcomes in White and Latino Lesbian, Gay, and Bisexual Young Adults," *Pediatrics* 2009; 123:346–52.

Chapter 16: Grace Land

1. This is one of the books of which Paul's authorship is in doubt.
2. James M. Washington, ed., *A Testament of Hope: The Essential Writings and Speeches of Martin Luther King Jr.* (New York: HarperOne, 1990), 284 and 286.
3. Paul Tillich, *The Shaking of Foundations* (New York: Charles Scribner's Sons, 1948), 162.